Big Book of NATURE

Stencil Designs

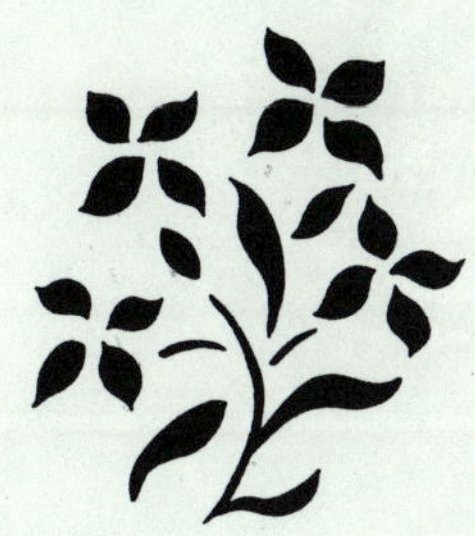

DOVER PUBLICATIONS, INC.
Mineola, New York

Published in Canada by General Publishing Company, Ltd., 30 Lesmill Road, Don Mills, Toronto, Ontario.
Published in the United Kingdom by Constable and Company, Ltd., 3 The Lanchesters, 162–164 Fulham Palace Road, London W6 9ER.

Bibliographical Note

Big Book of Nature Stencil Designs is a new work, first published by Dover Publications, Inc., in 1997. For a complete list of the sources of the designs in this book, see p. 92.

DOVER *Pictorial Archive* SERIES

This book belongs to the Dover Pictorial Archive Series. You may use the designs and illustrations for graphics and crafts applications, free and without special permission, provided that you include no more than ten in the same publication or project. (For permission for additional use, please write to: Permissions Department, Dover Publications, Inc., 31 East 2nd Street, Mineola, N.Y. 11501.)
However, republication or reproduction of any illustration by any other graphic service, whether it be in a book or in any other design resource, is strictly prohibited.

International Standard Book Number: 0-486-29777-2

Manufactured in the United States of America
Dover Publications, Inc., 31 East 2nd Street, Mineola, N.Y. 11501

Publisher's Note

Stenciling is a decorative technique that has been practised the world over for centuries. Aside from their use in decorating walls, floors, furniture, textiles, and countless other practical applications, stencil designs are ideally suited for direct graphic use in books, periodicals, catalogs, newsletters, stationery and a host of other print projects.

This treasury of nature stencil designs, conveniently arranged by topic, brings together the work of several artists and includes a rich range of styles and approaches. Use these designs without fee or permission in art, craft, and design projects.

Contents

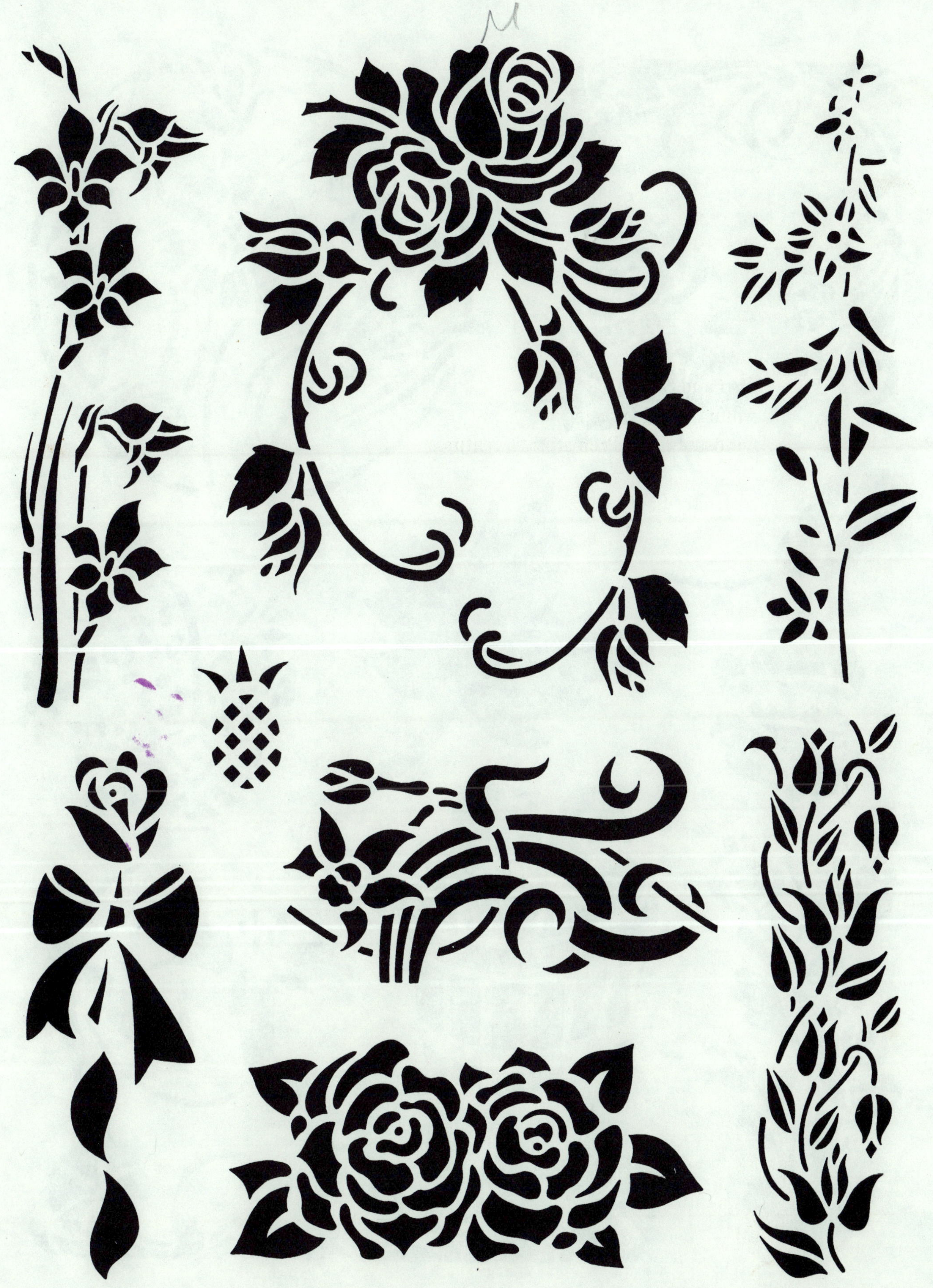

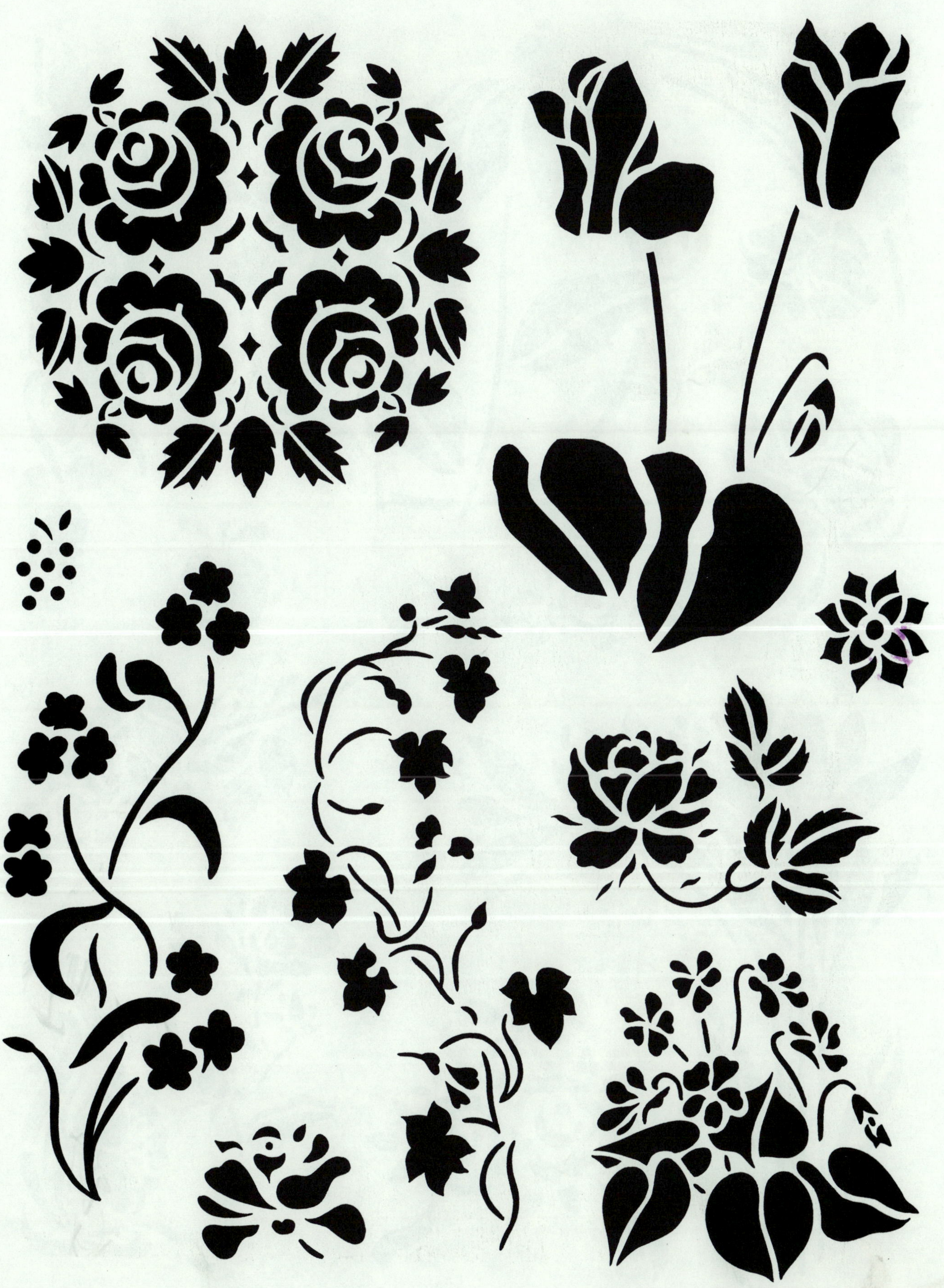

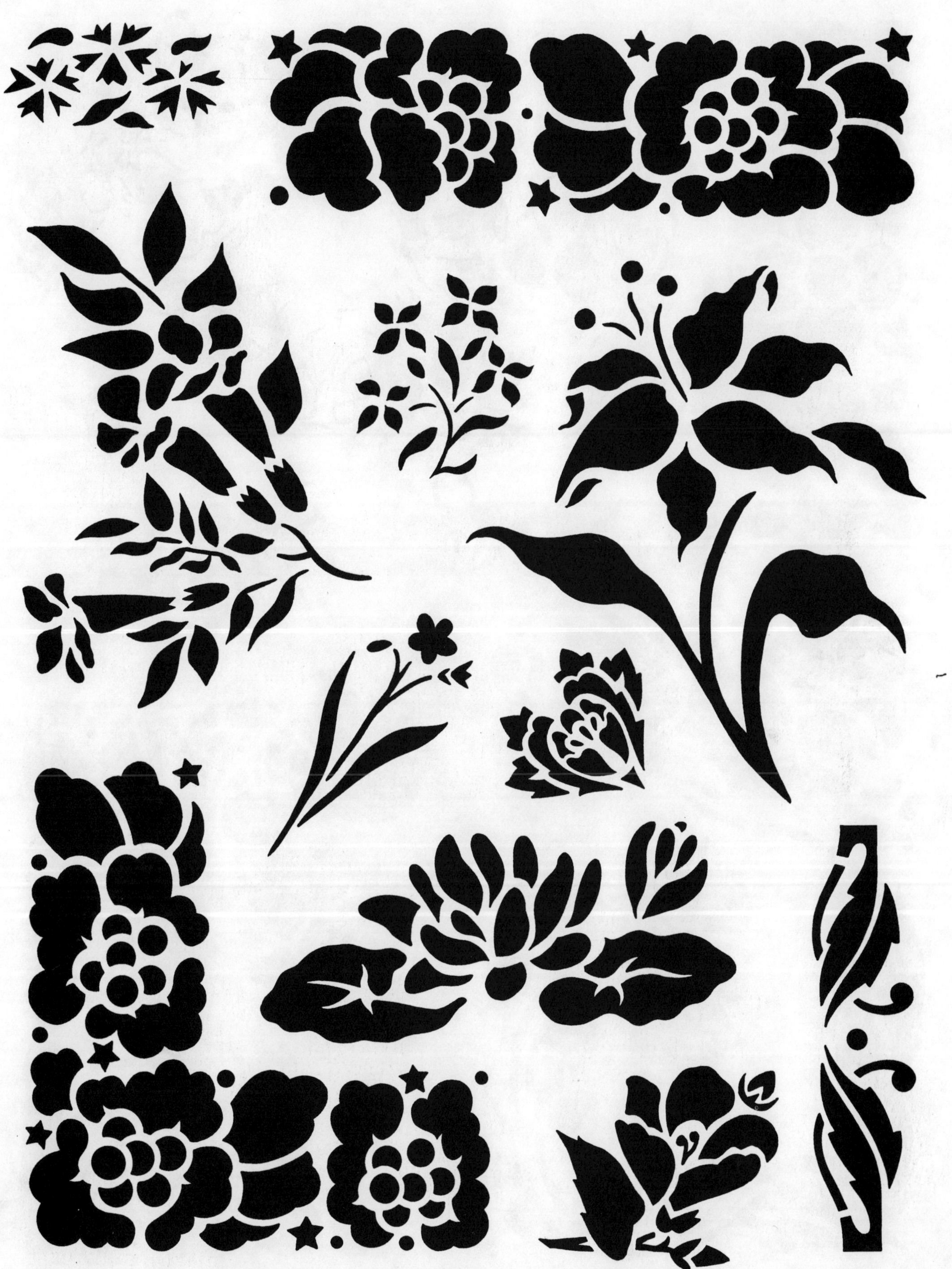

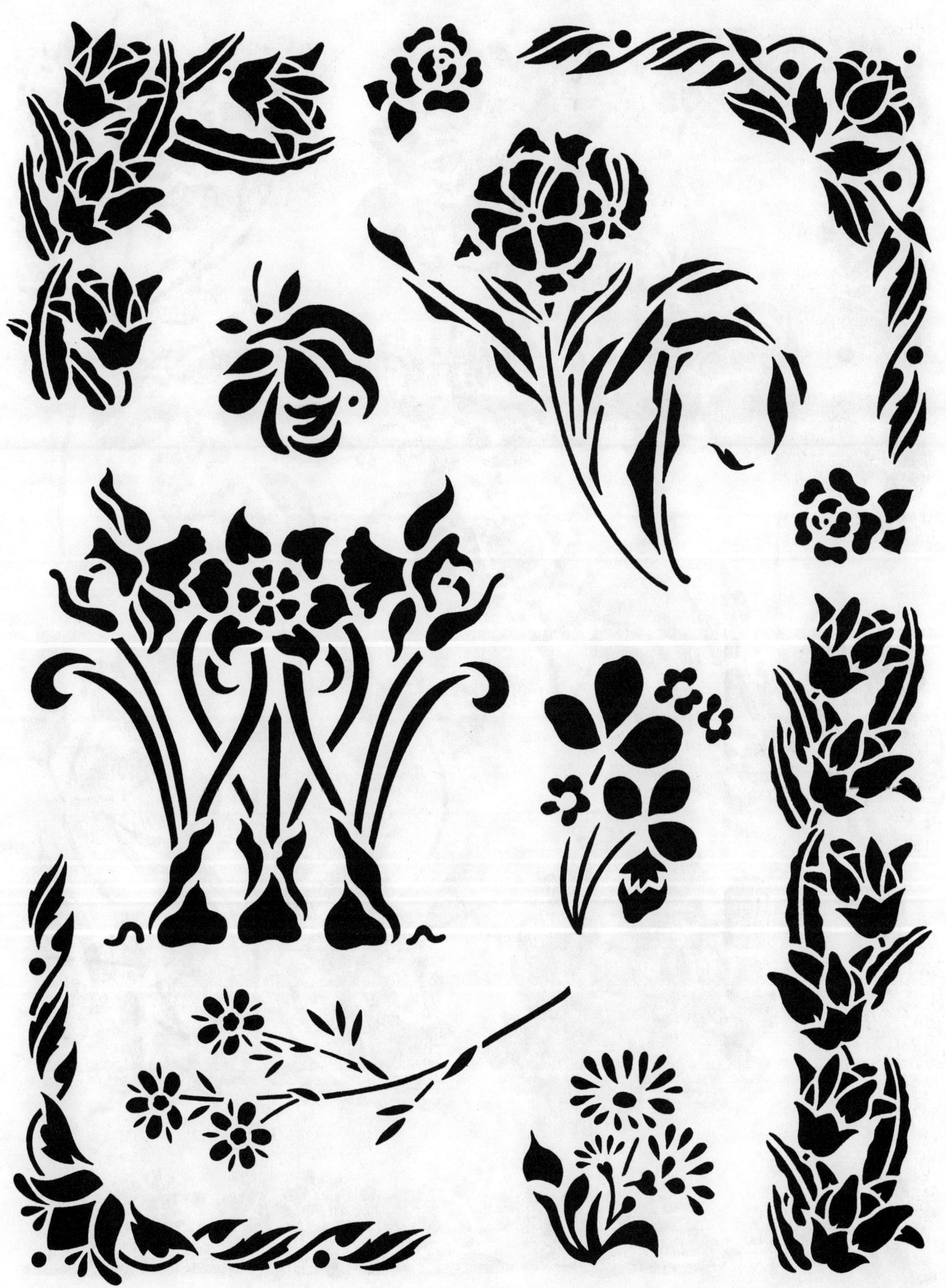

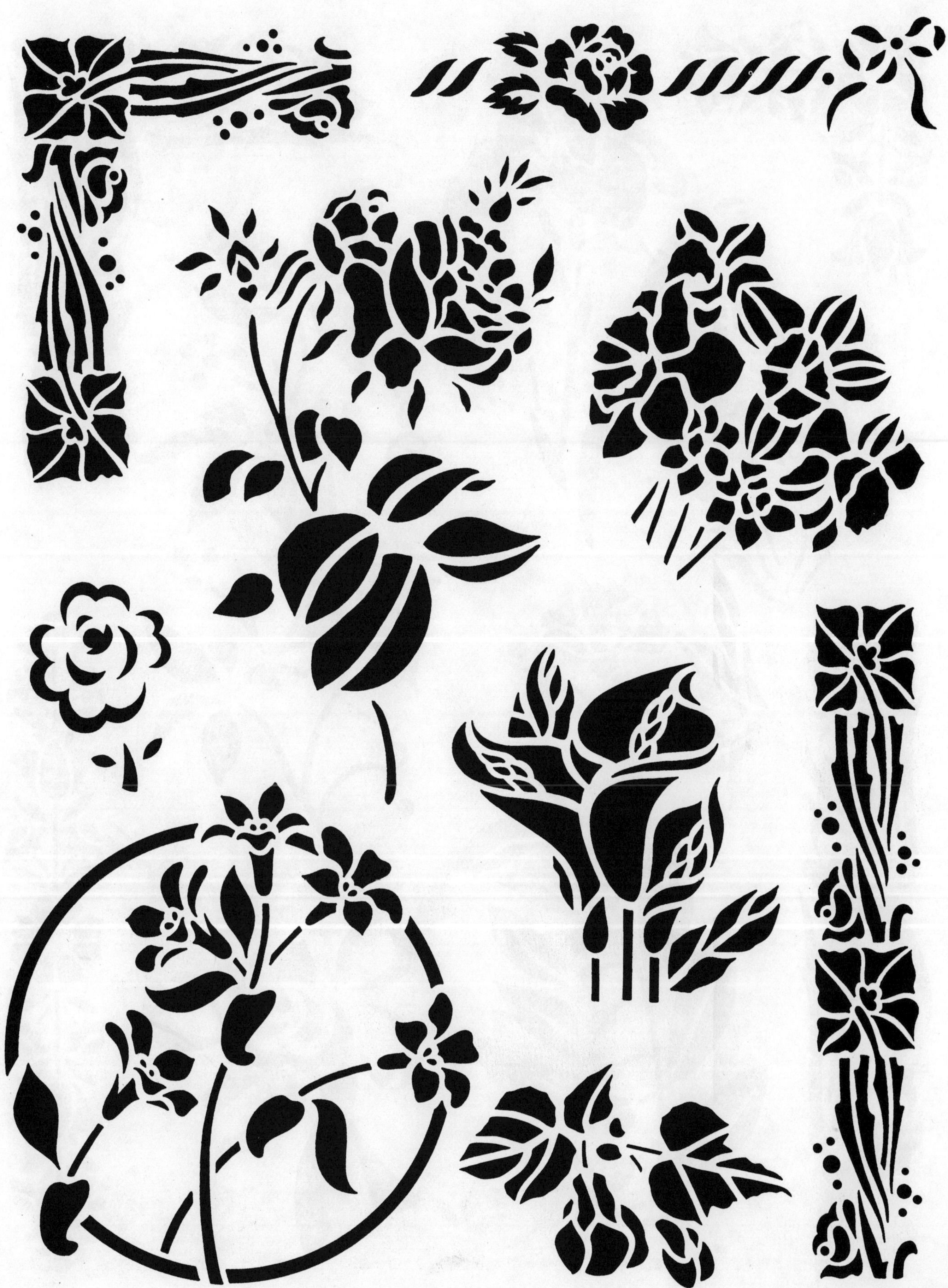

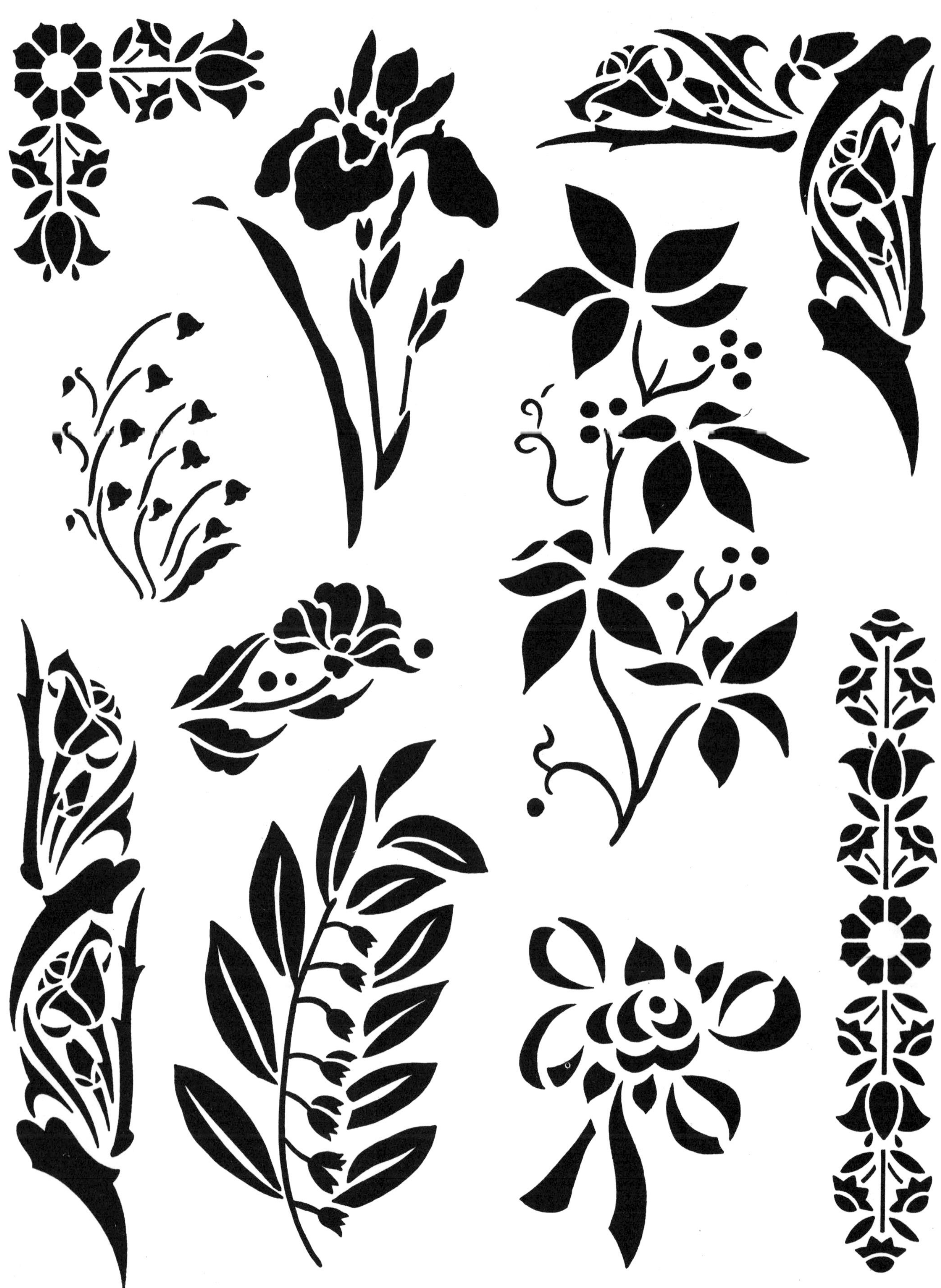

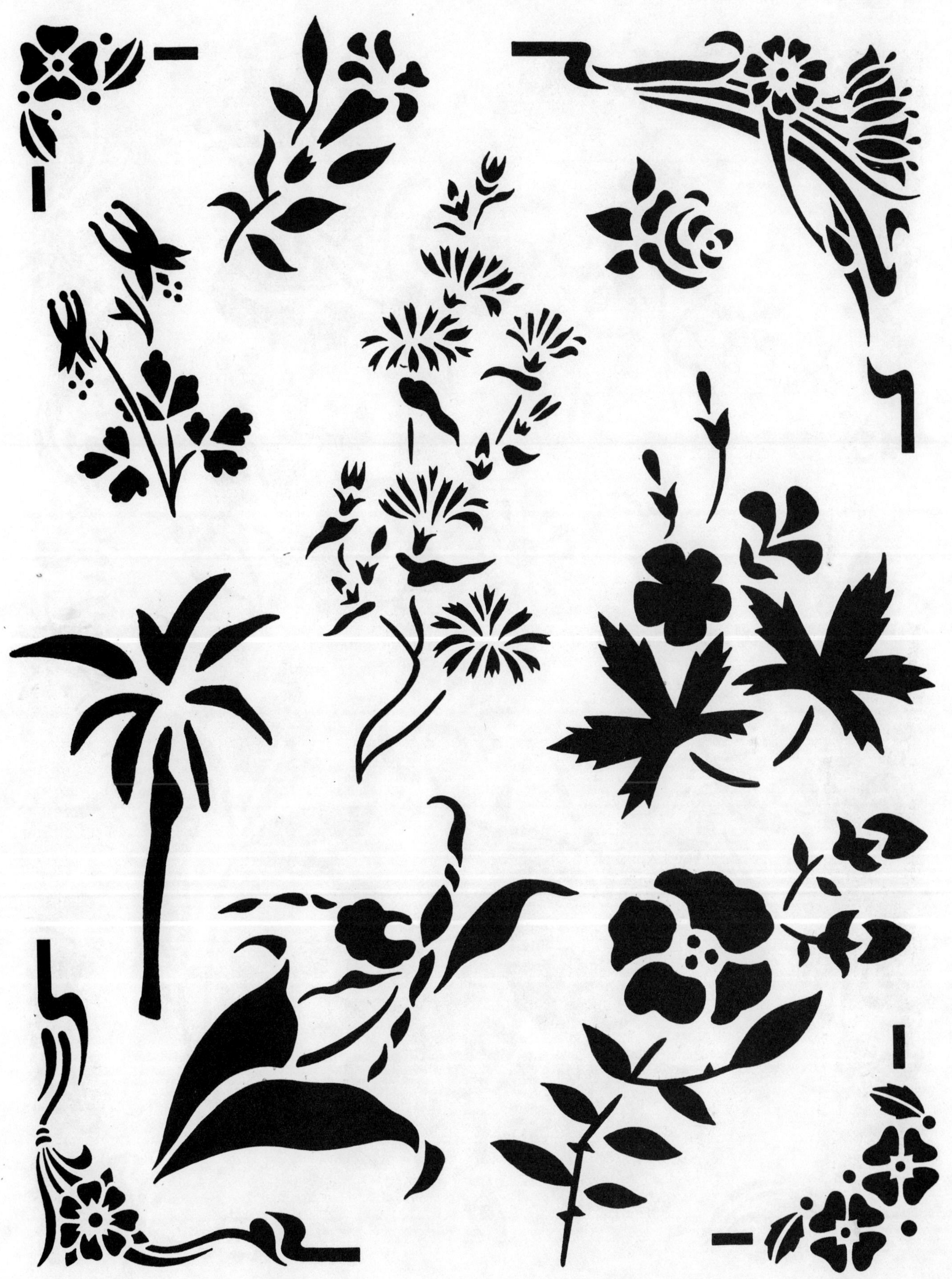

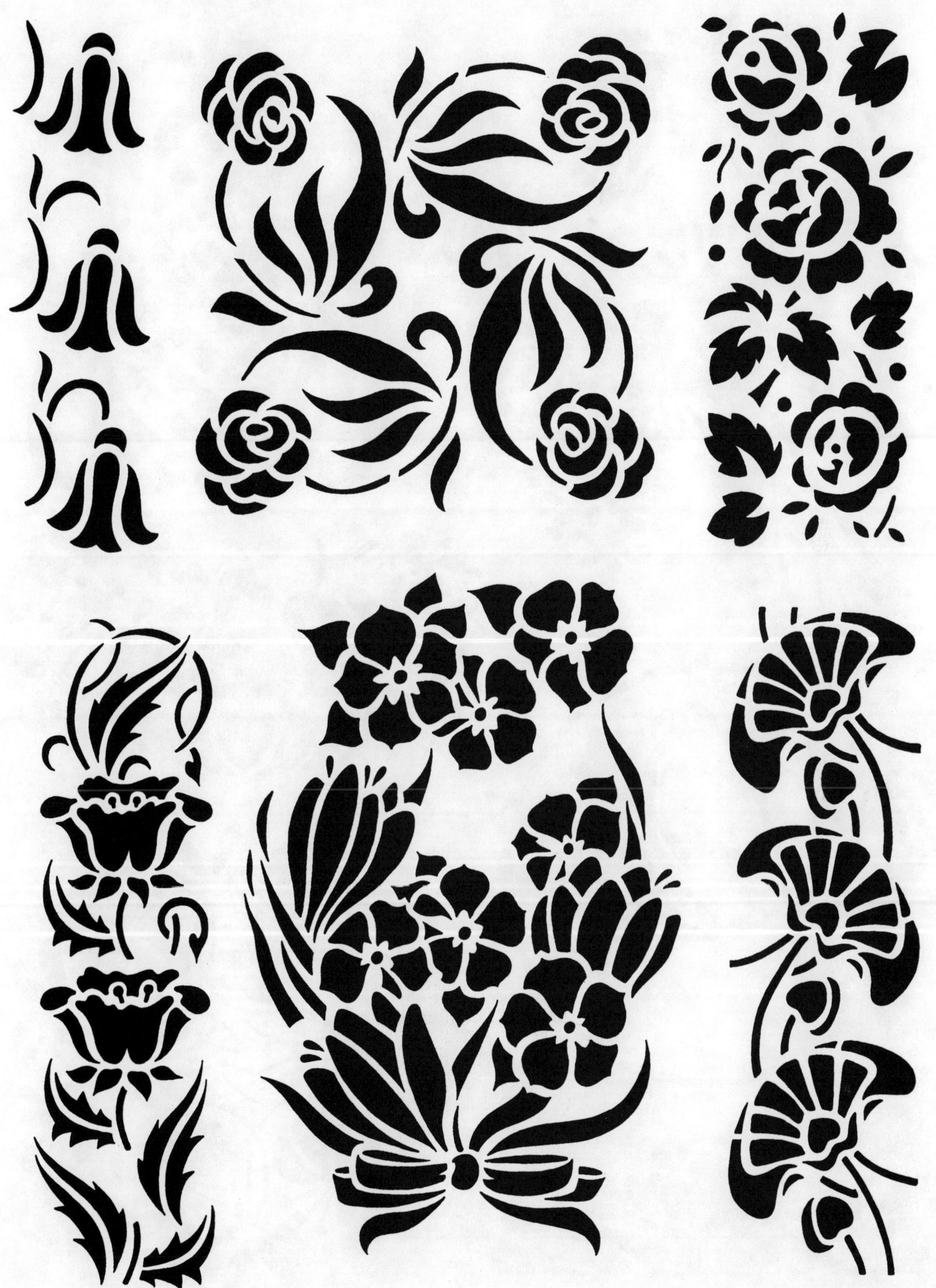

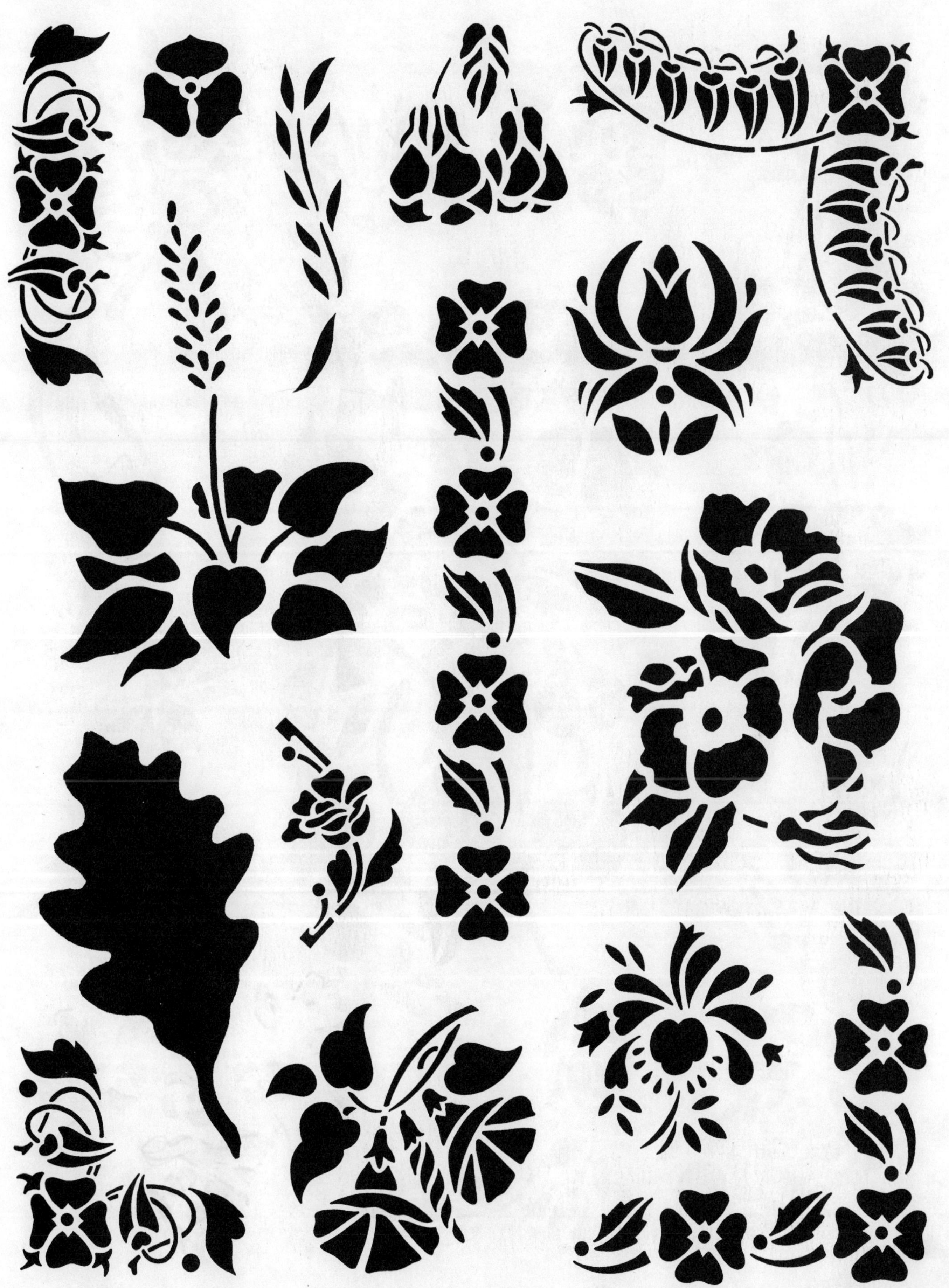

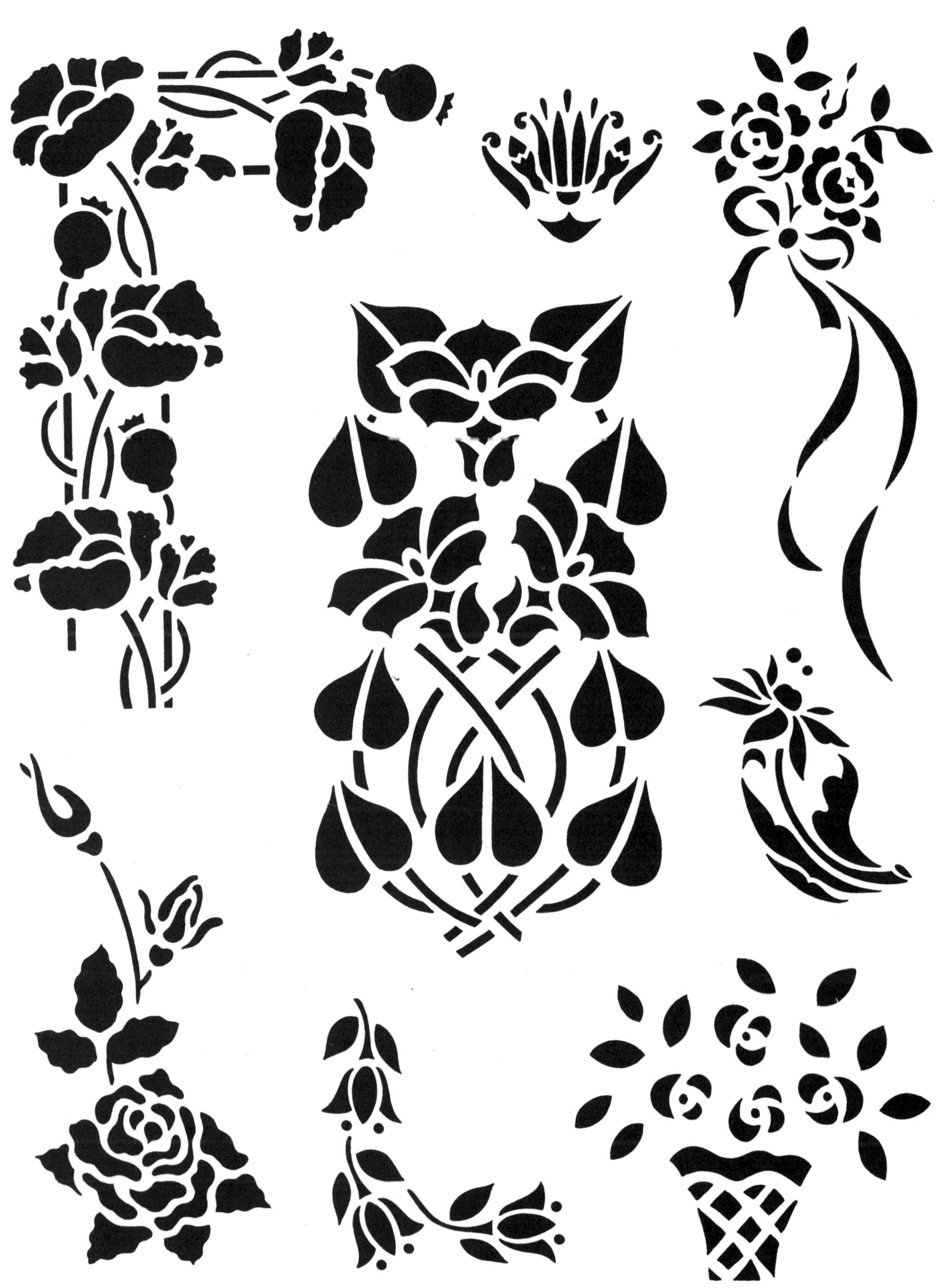

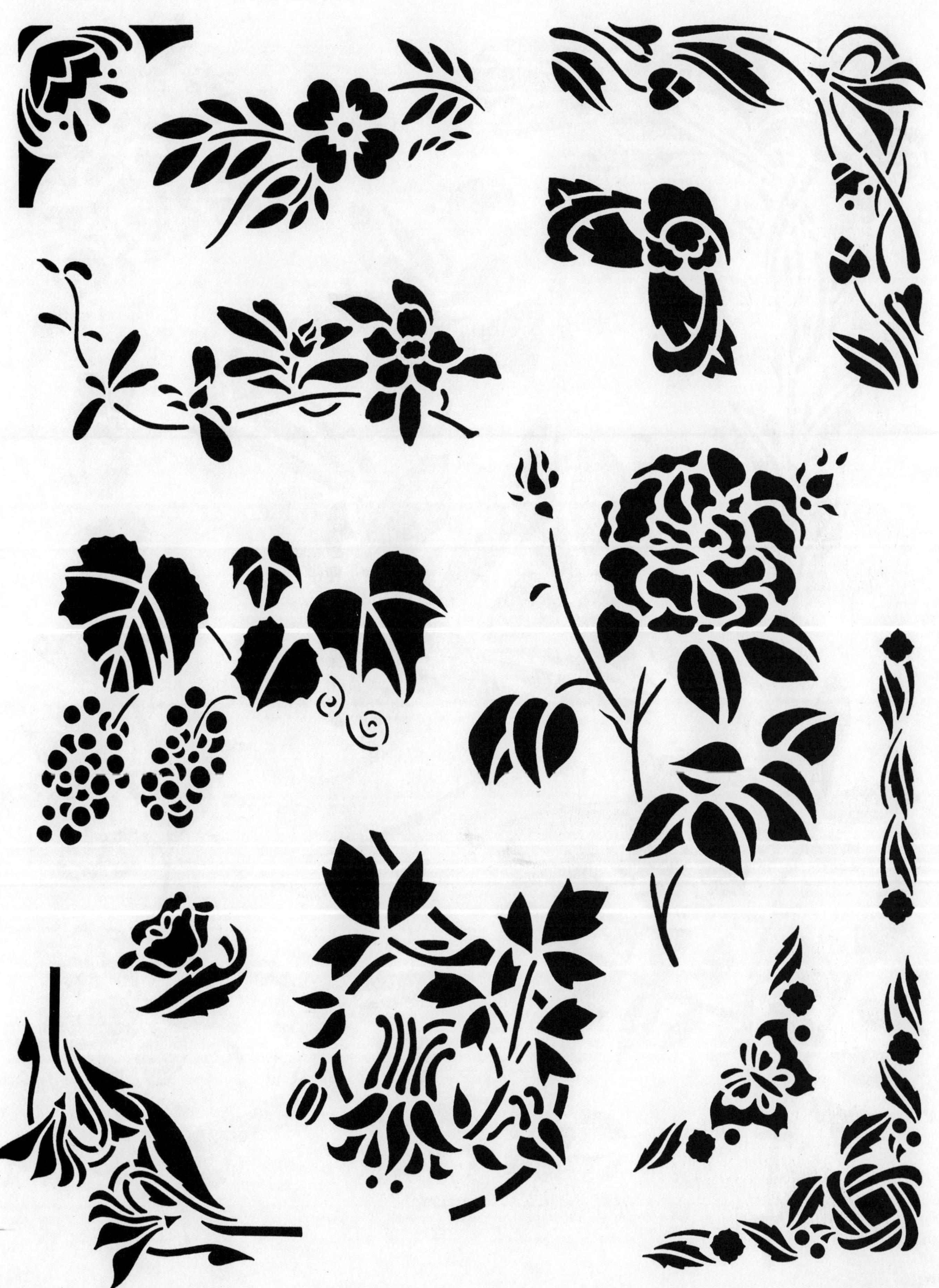

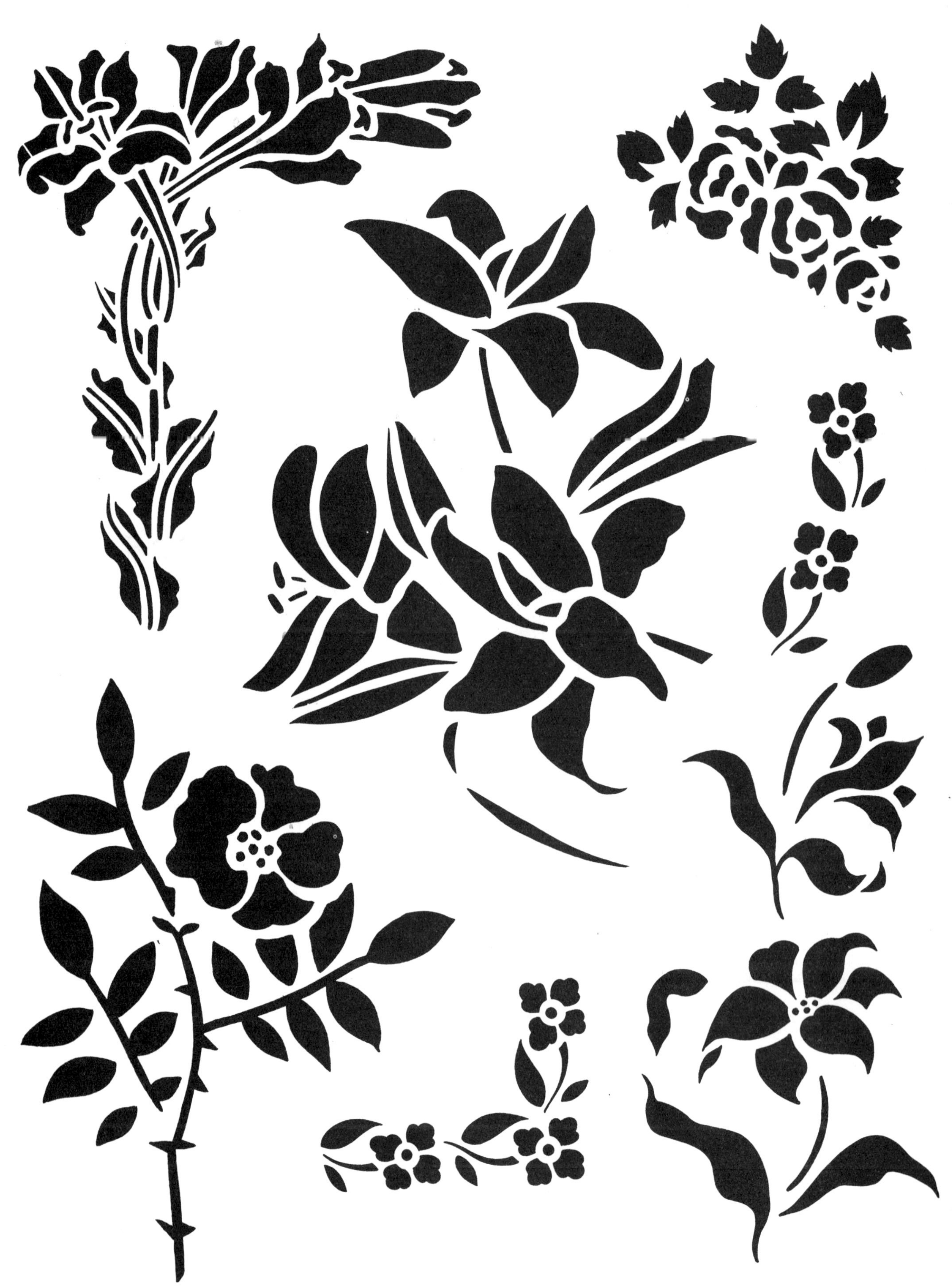

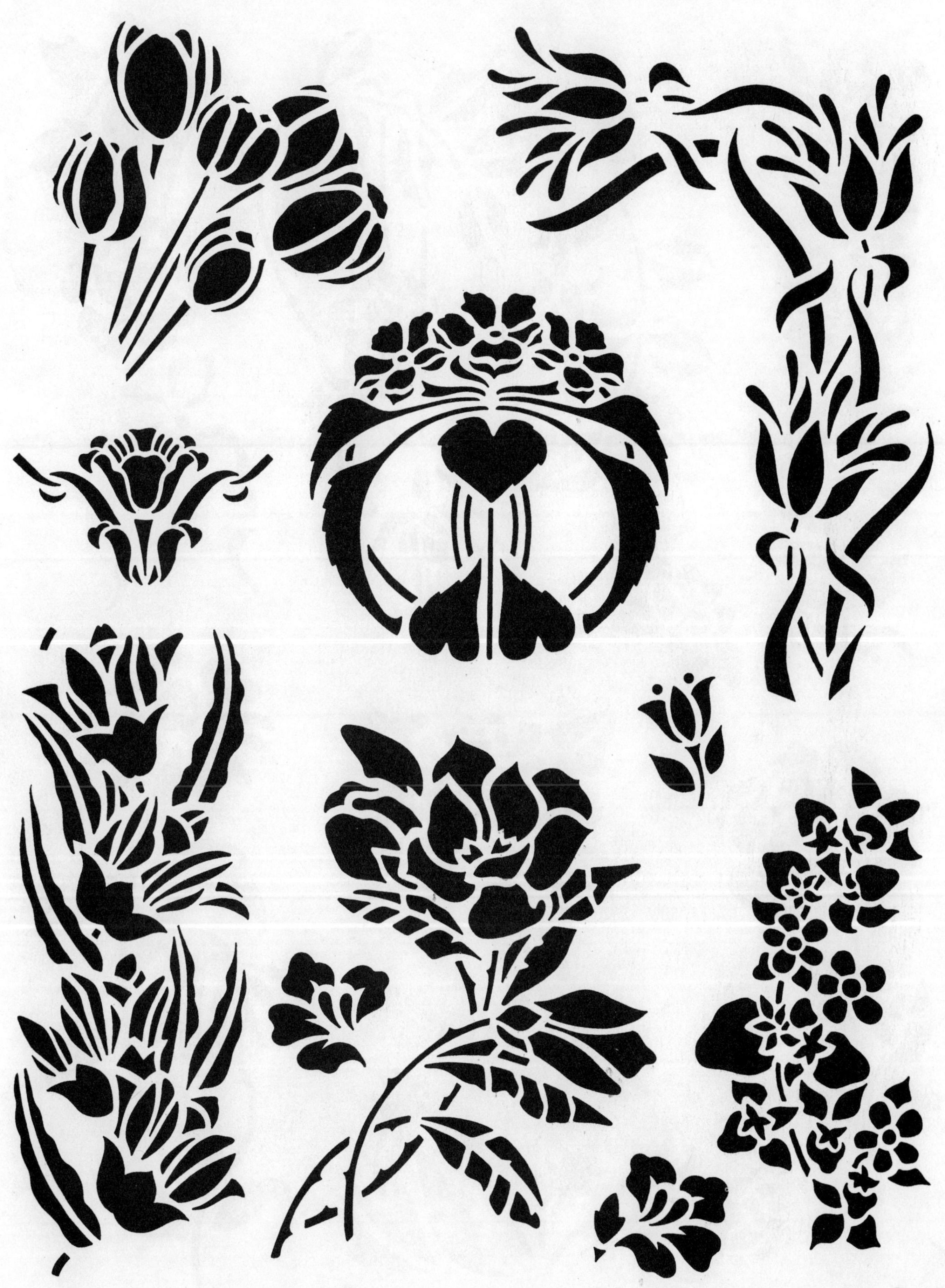

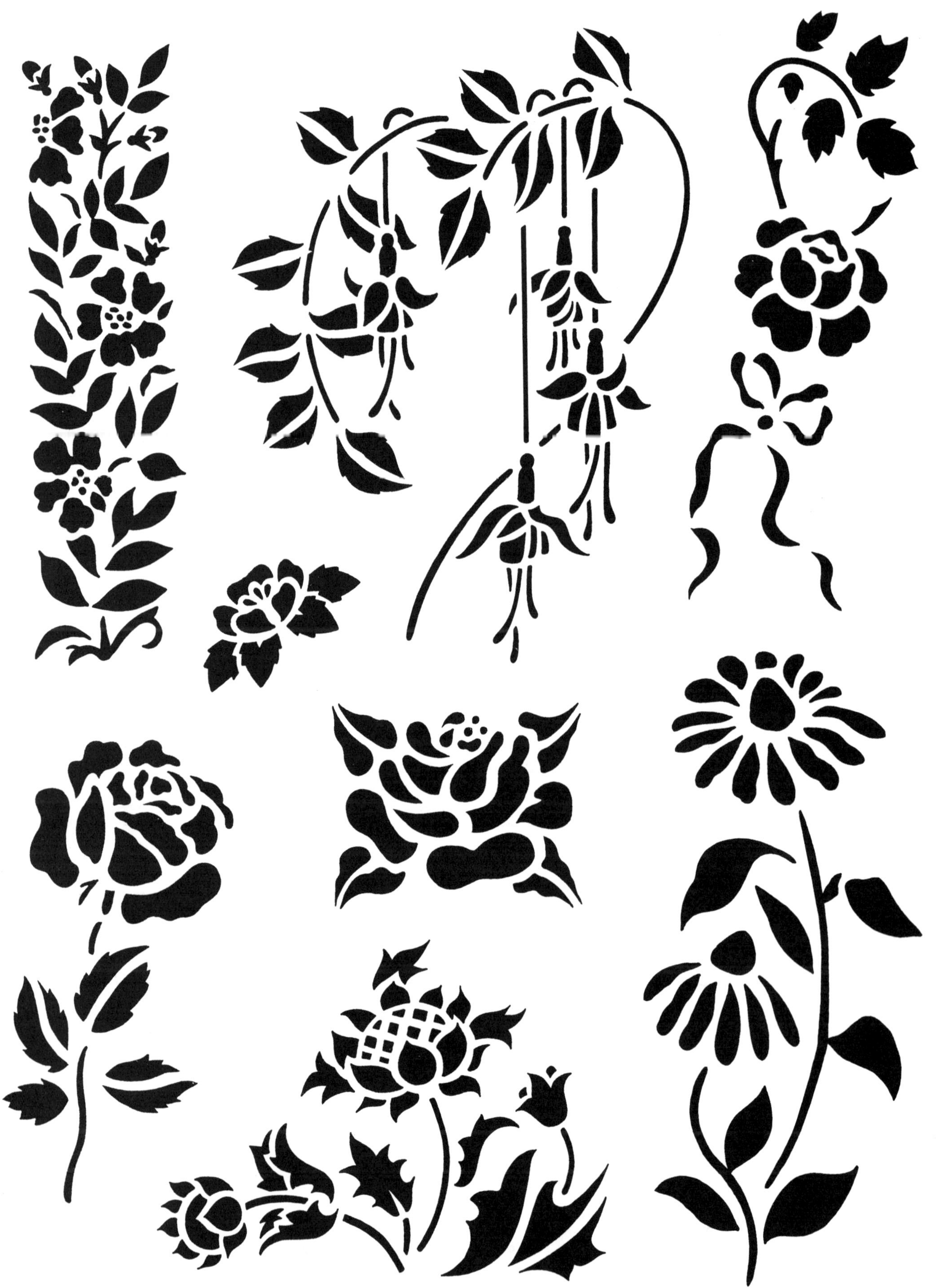

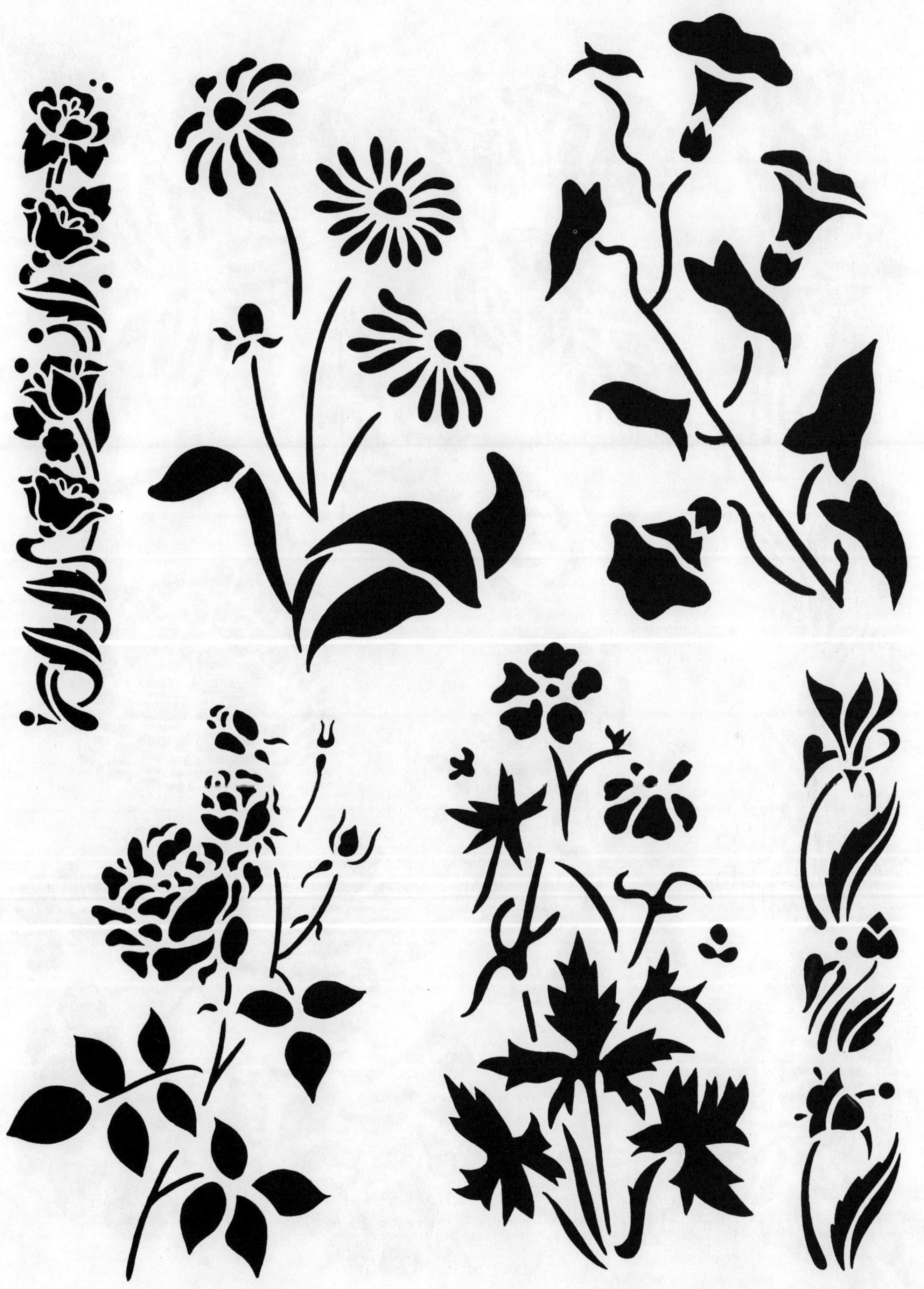

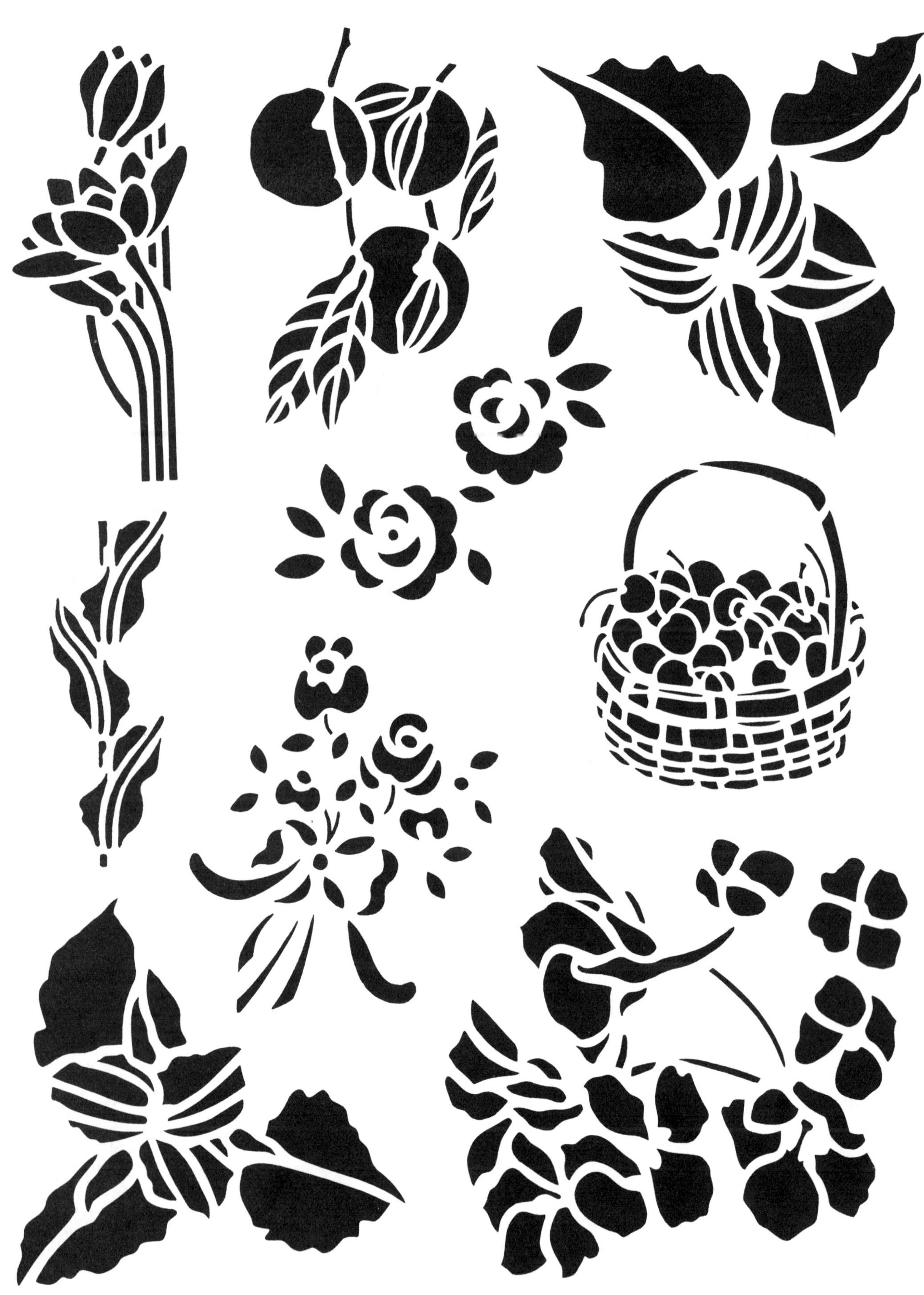

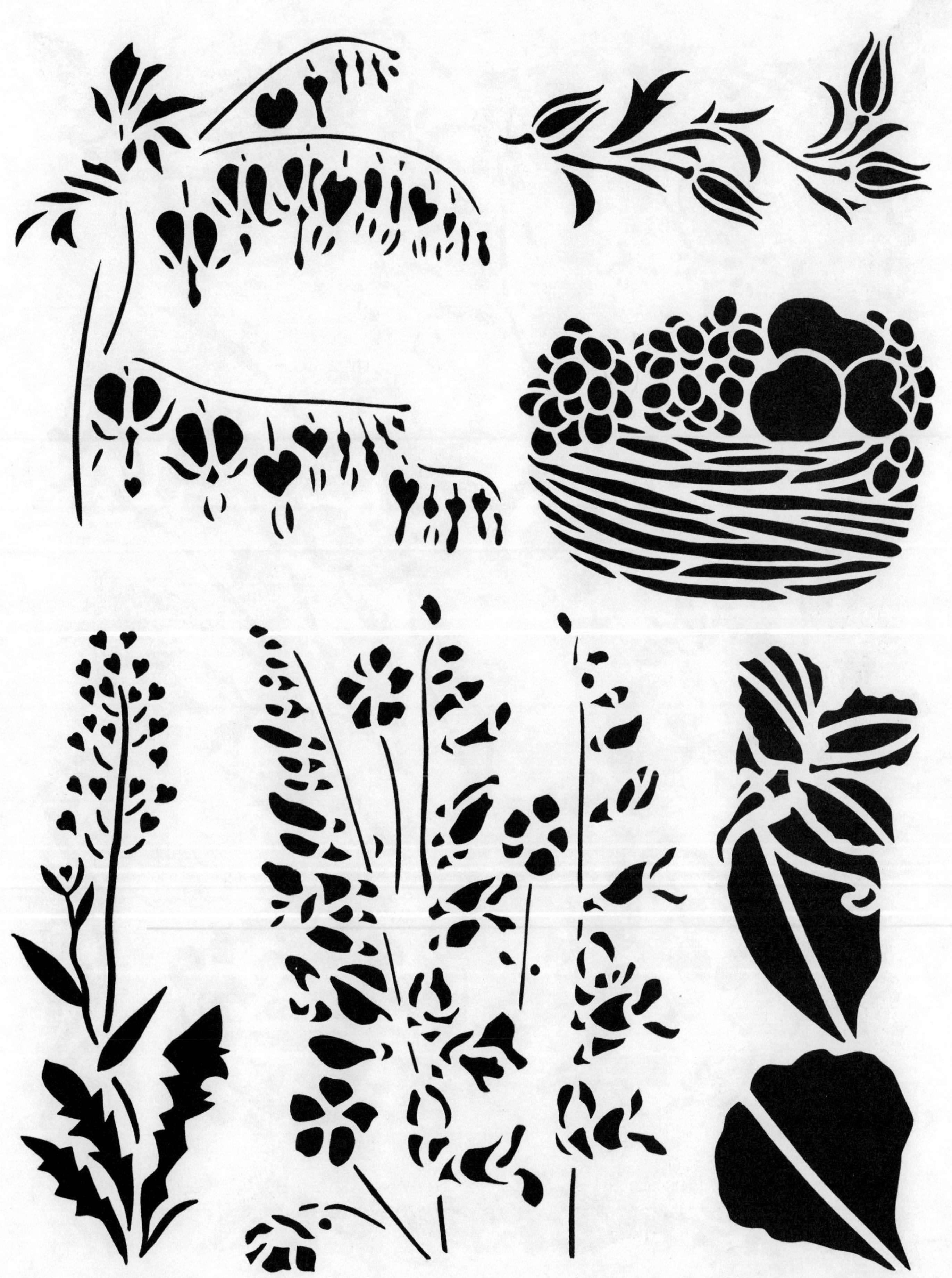

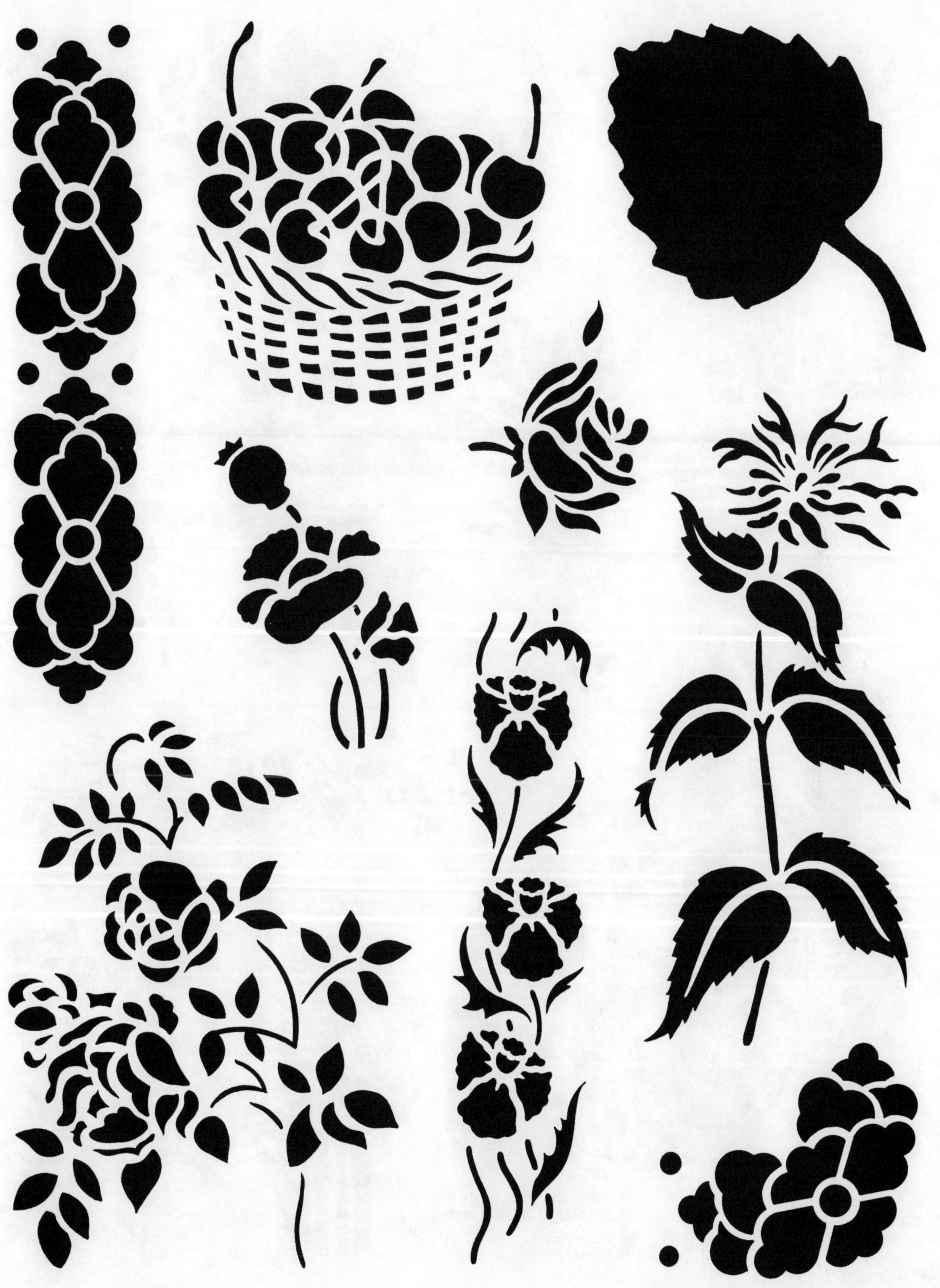

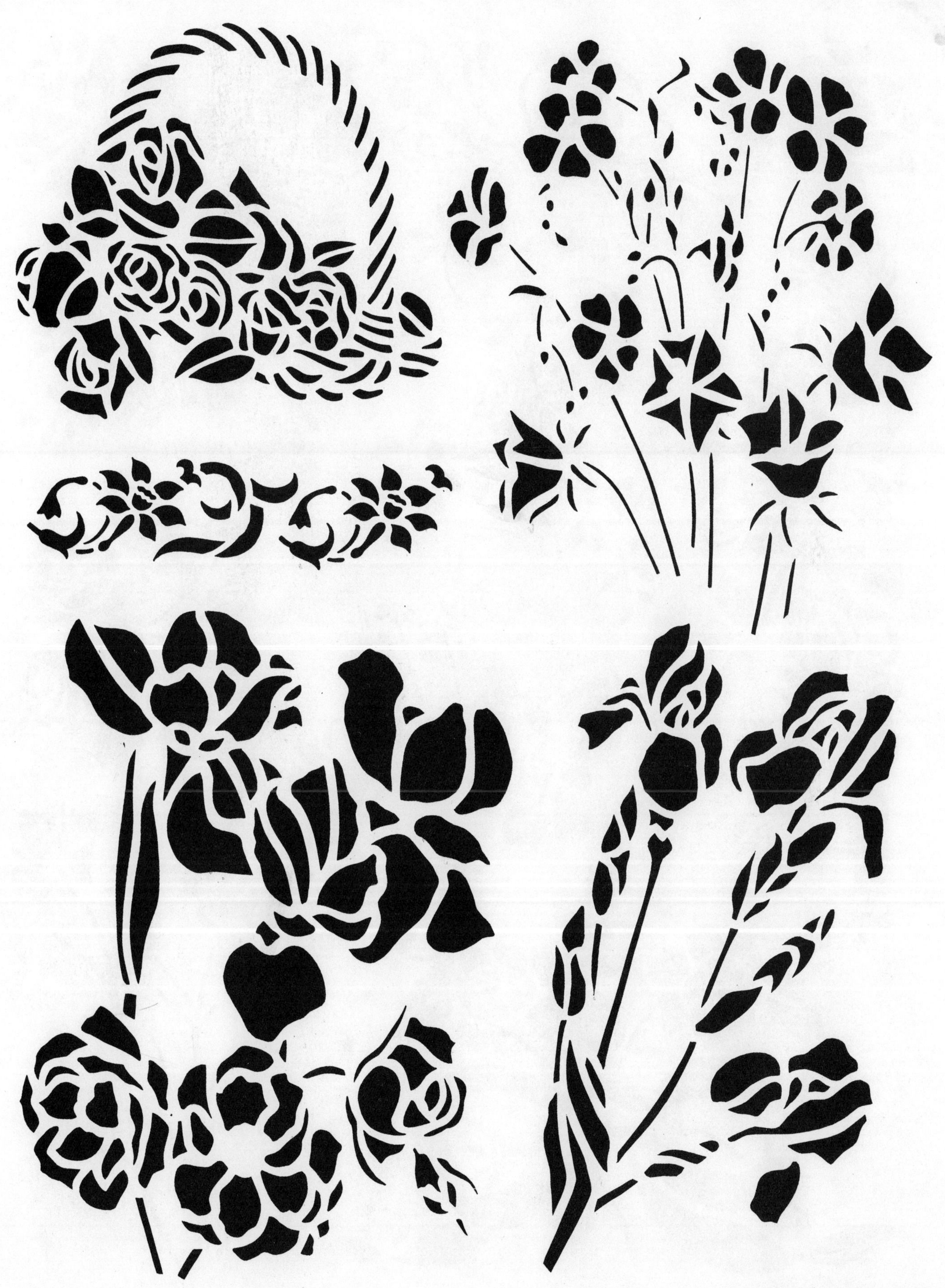

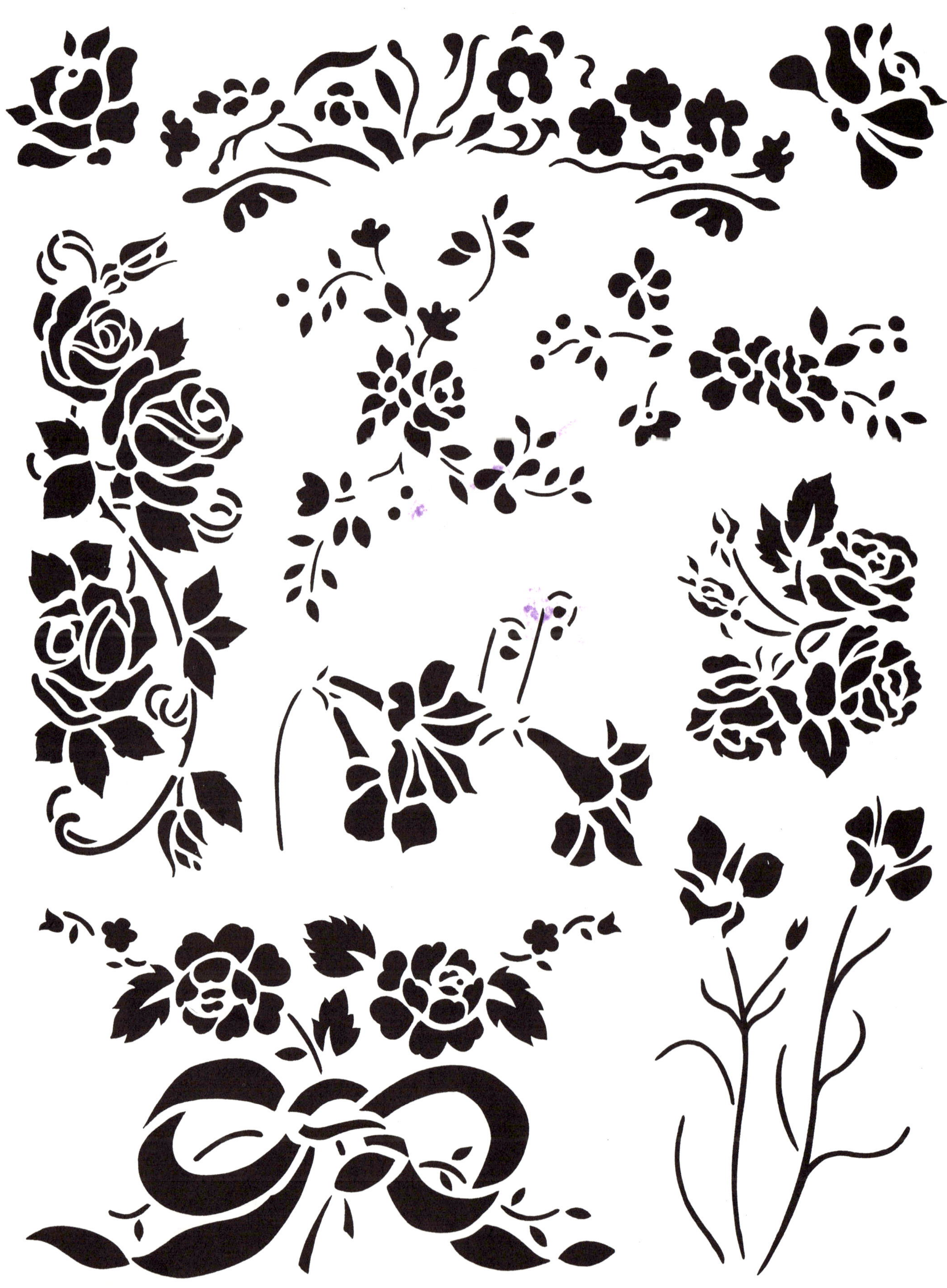

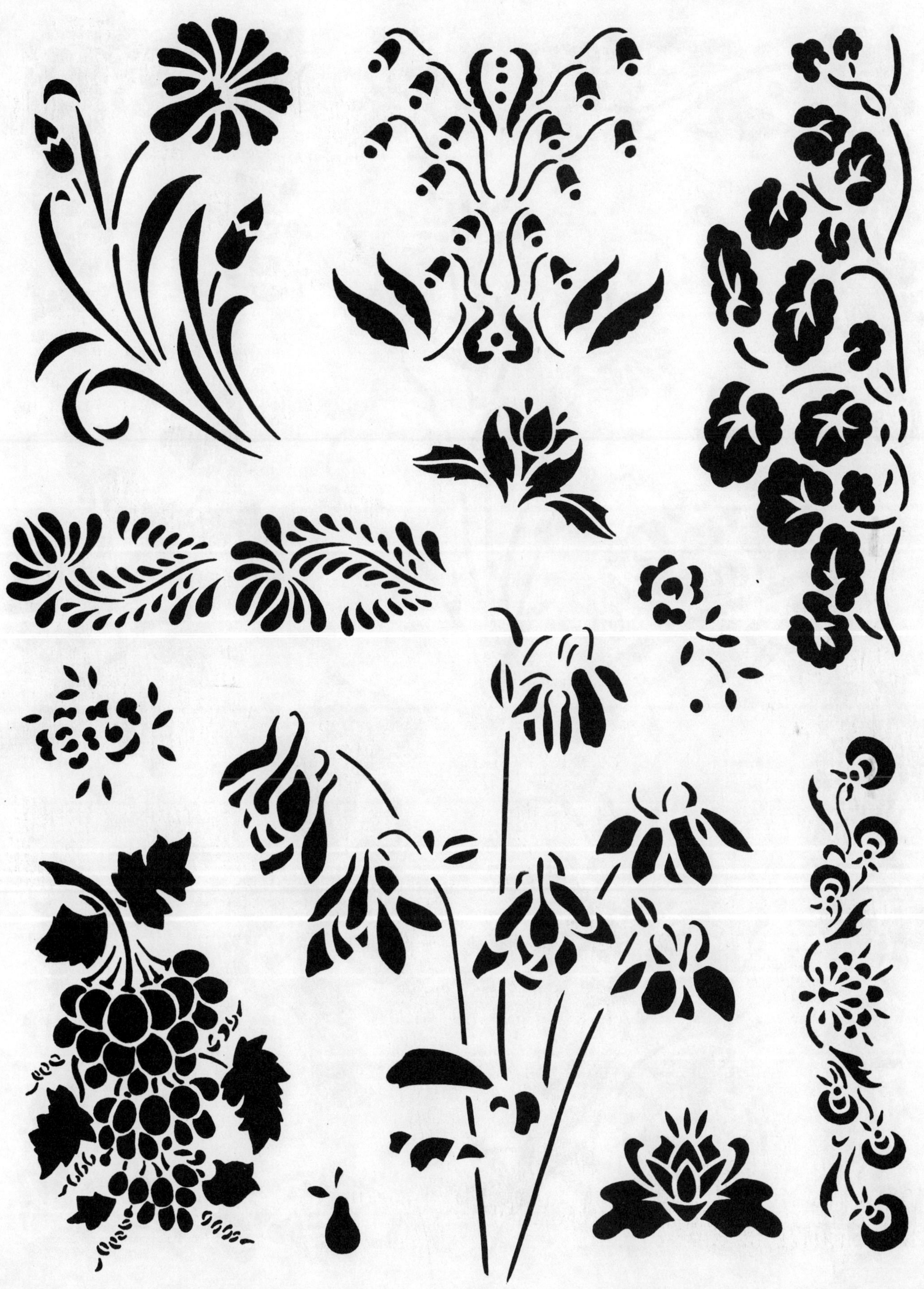

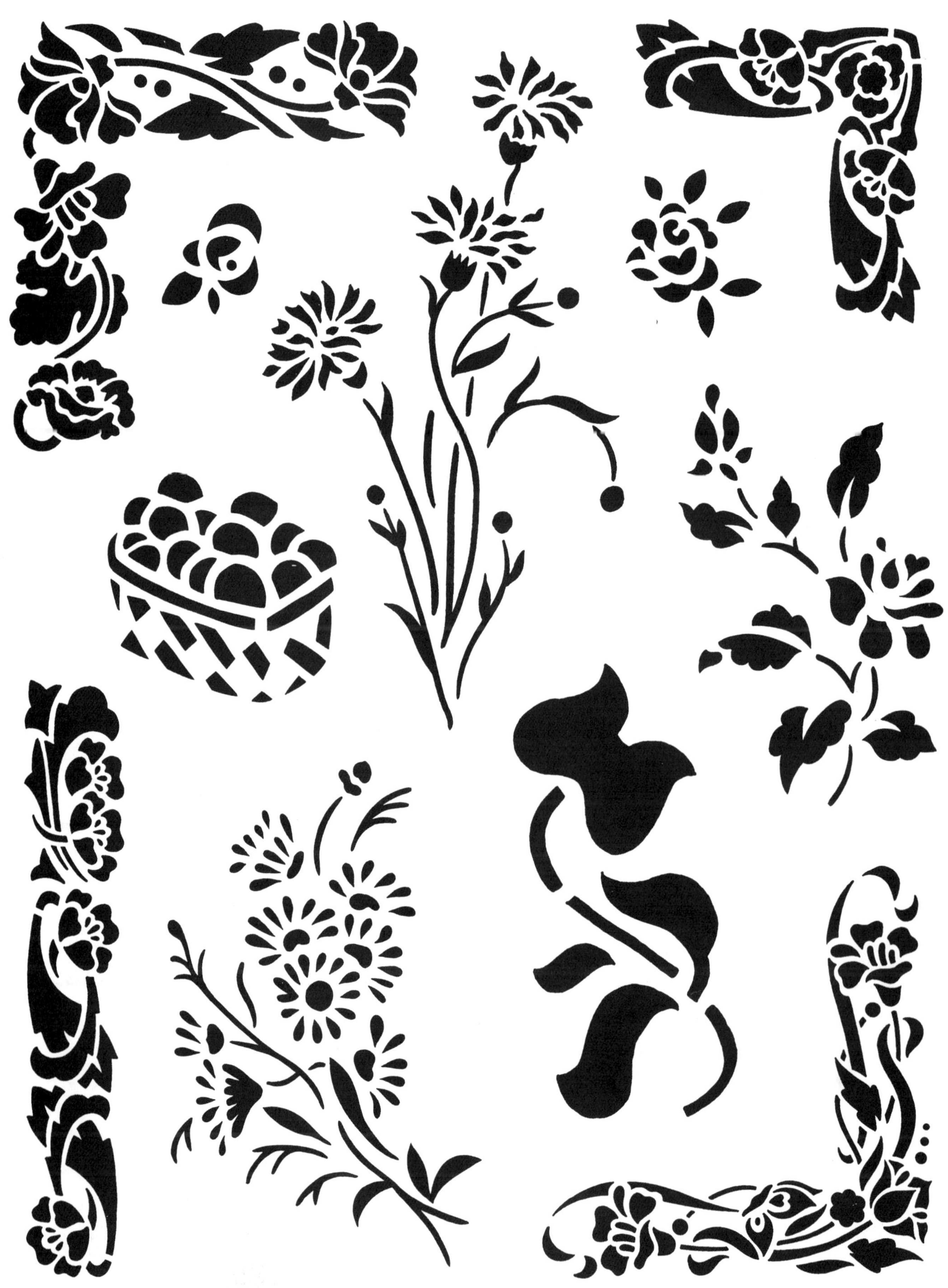

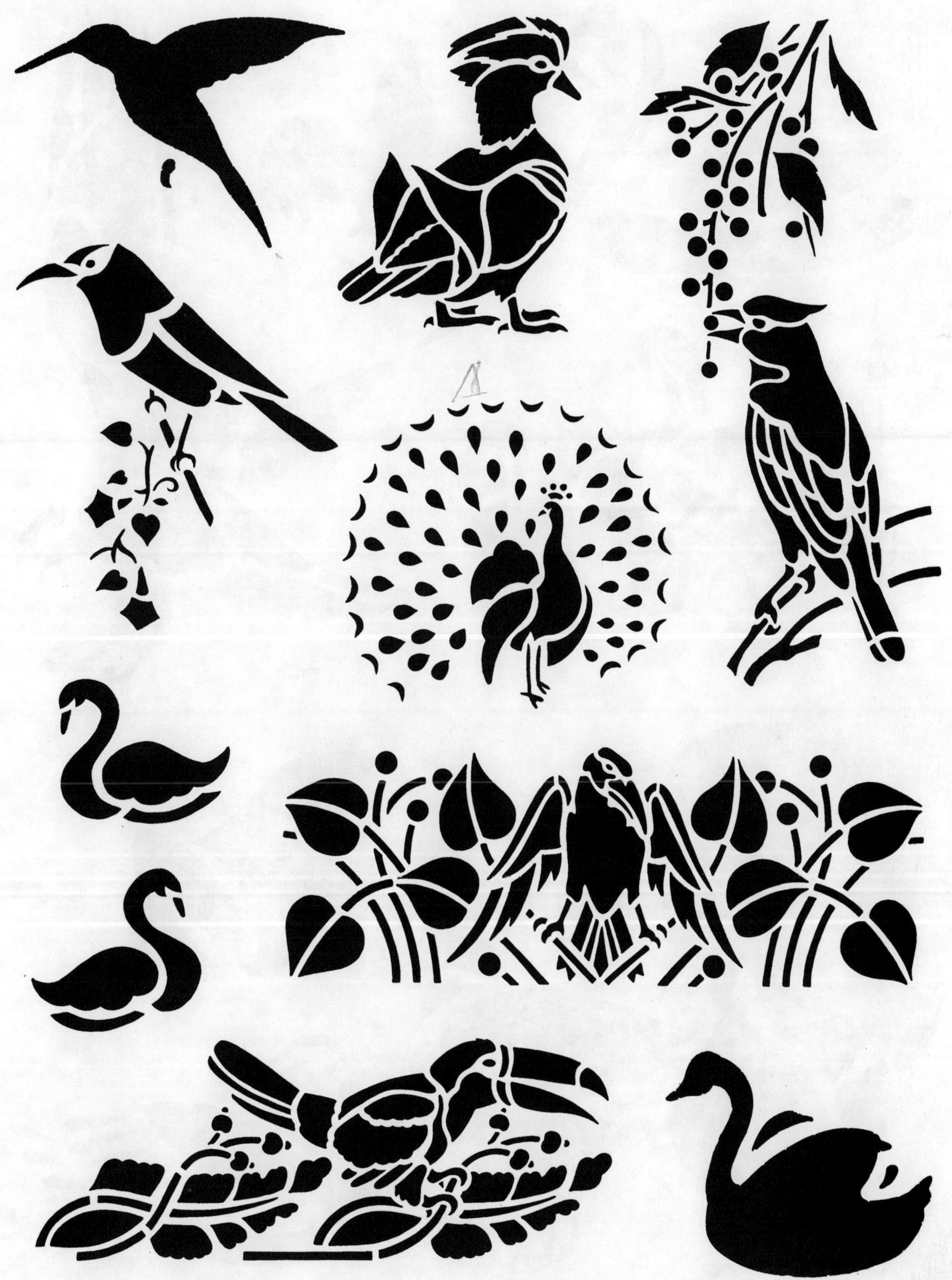

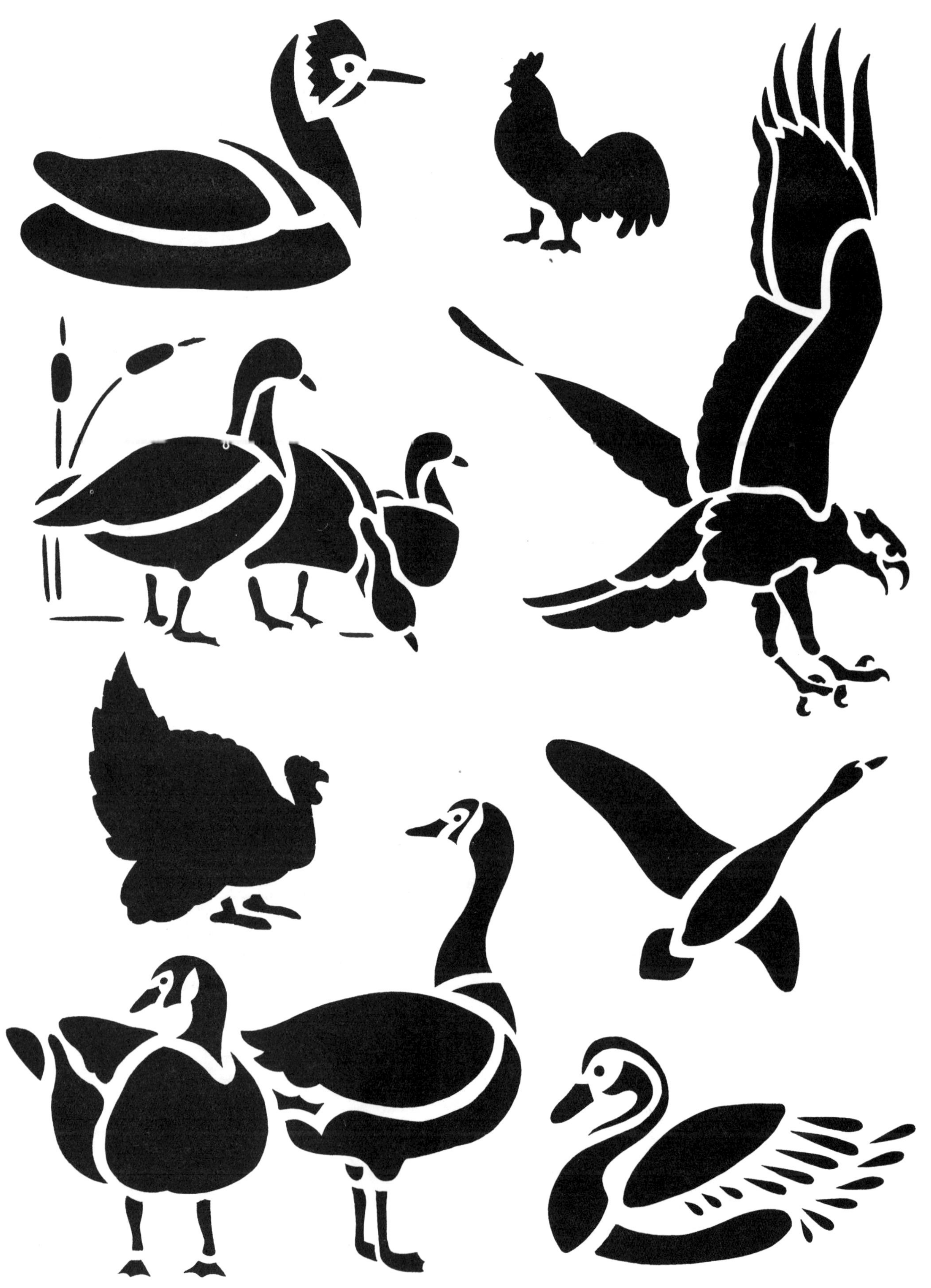

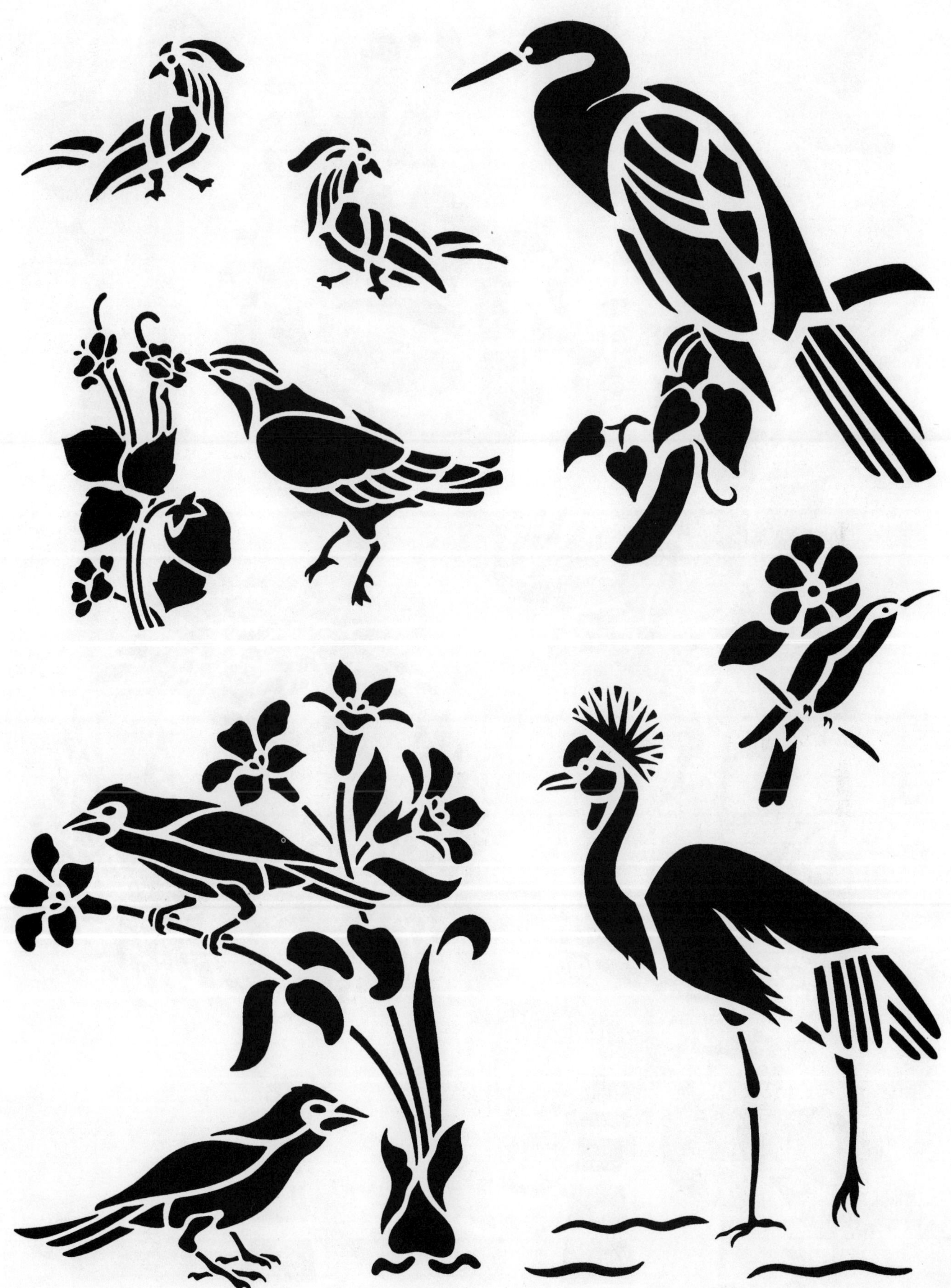

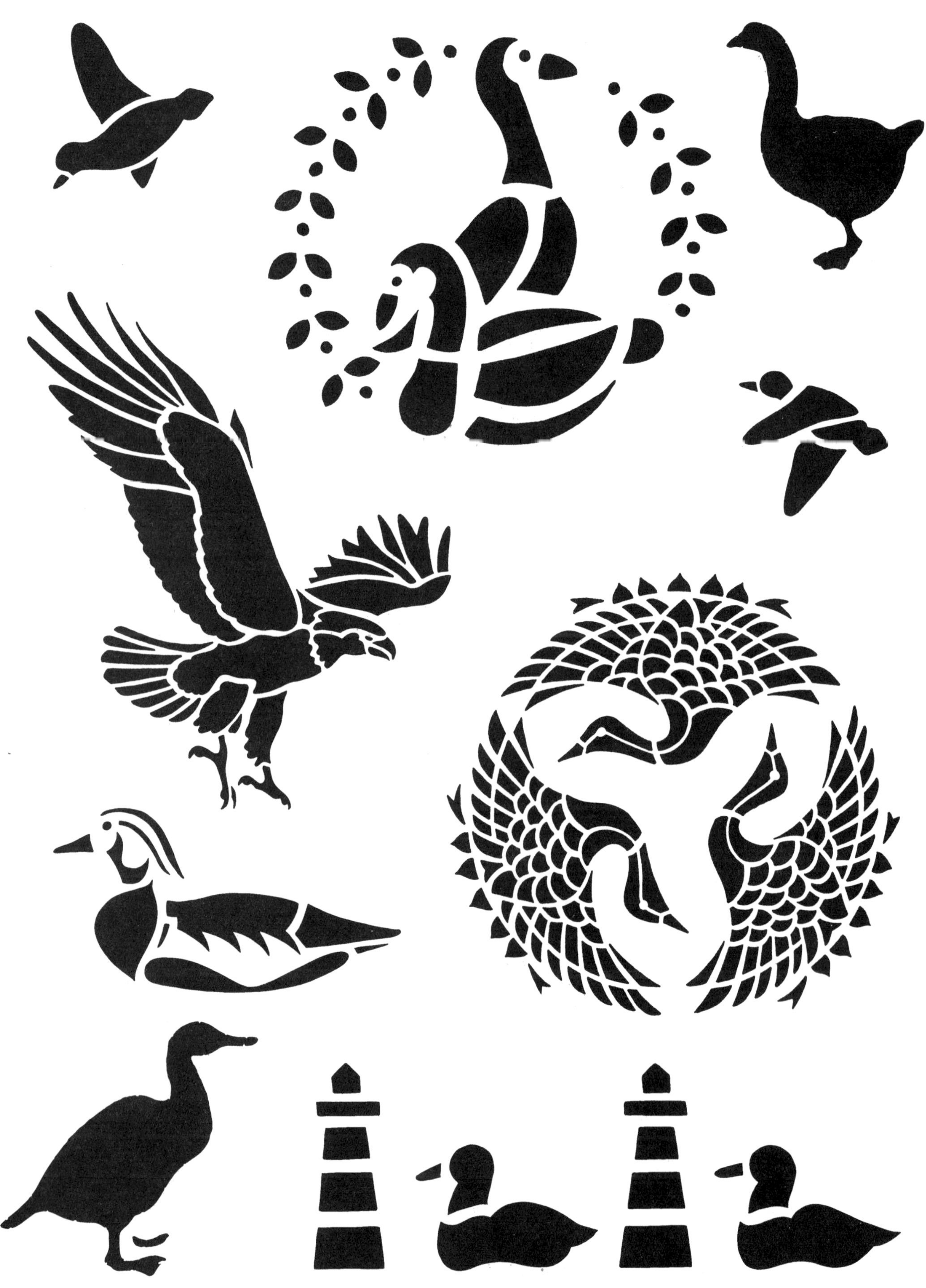

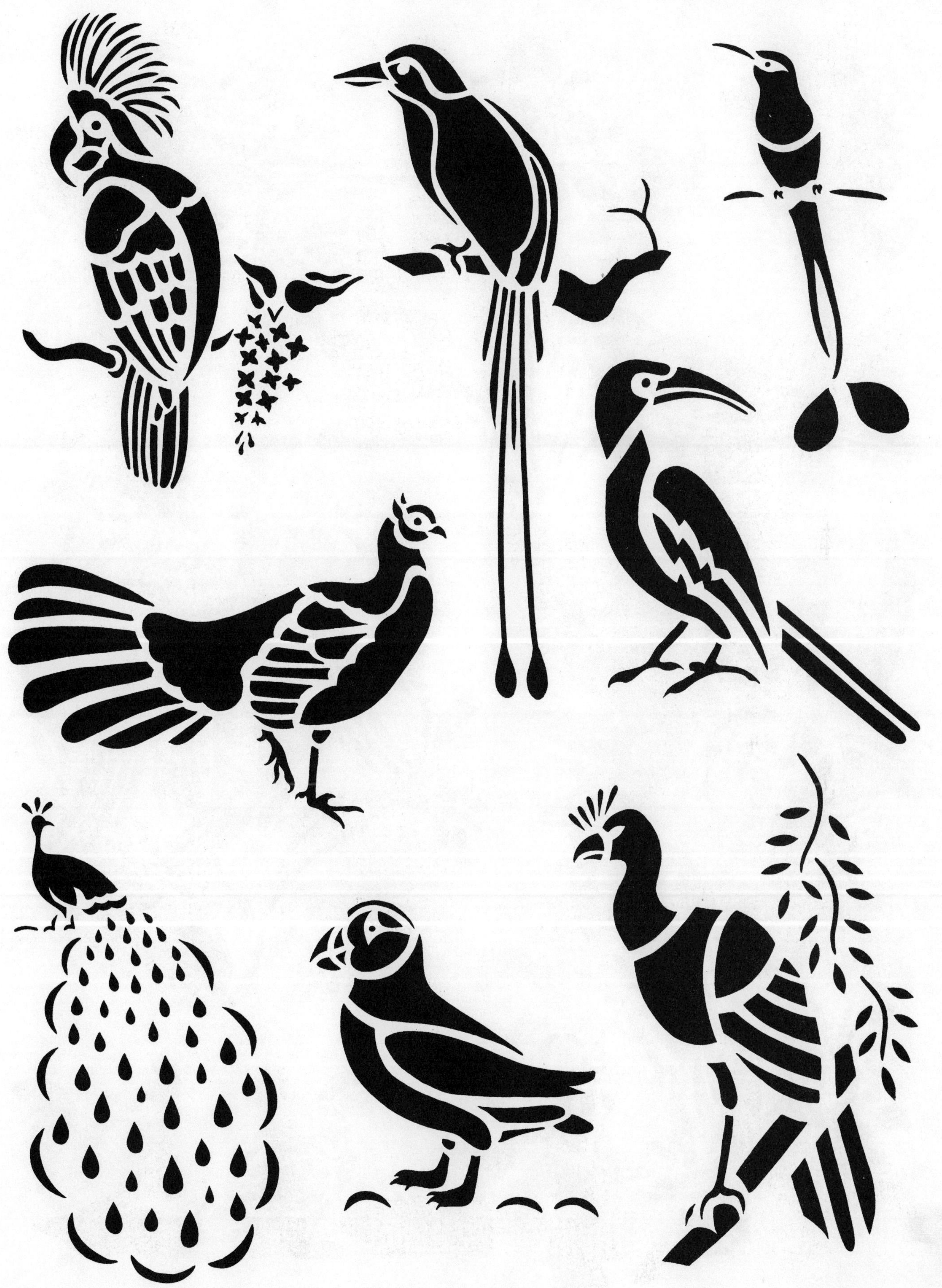

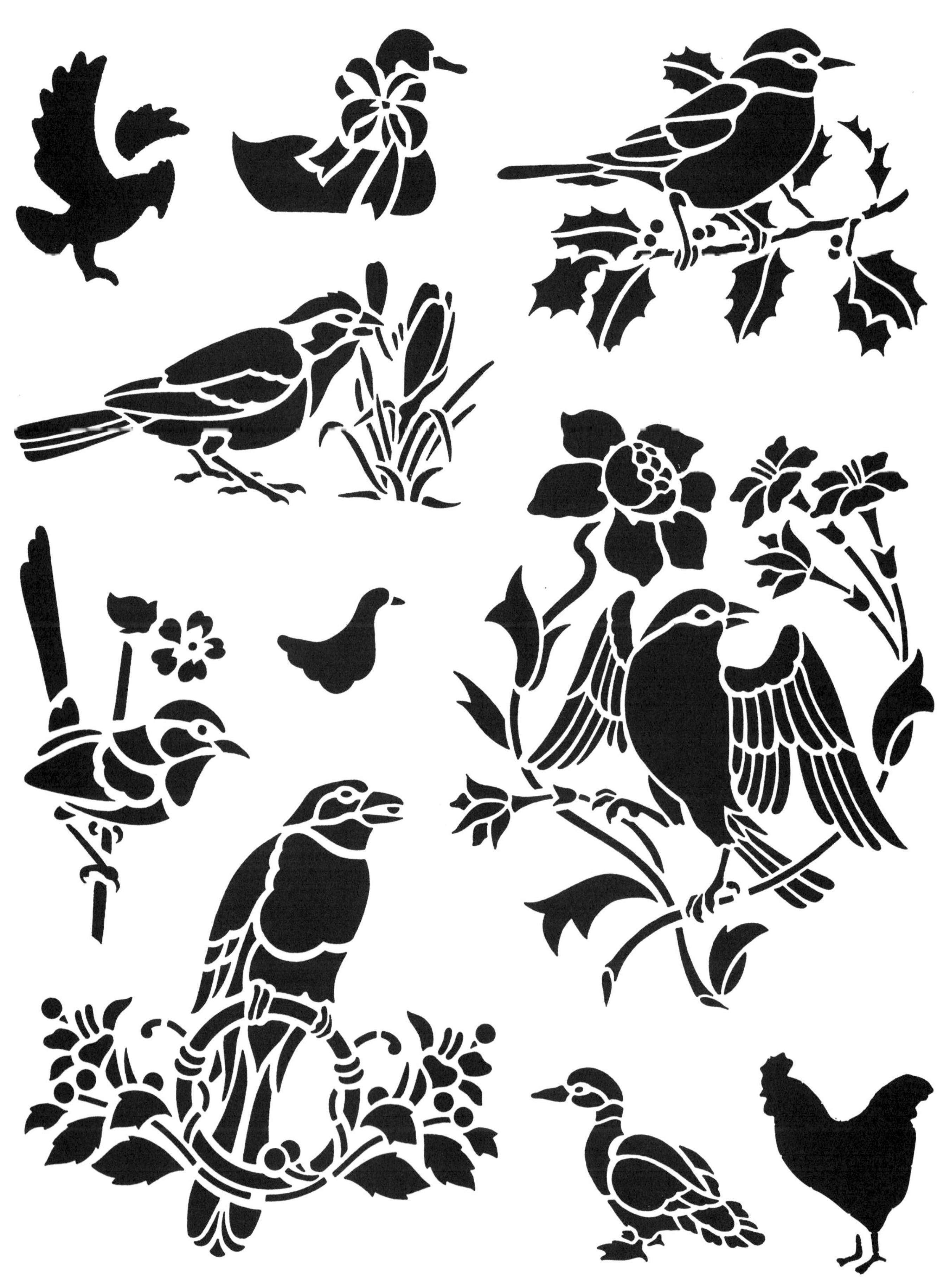

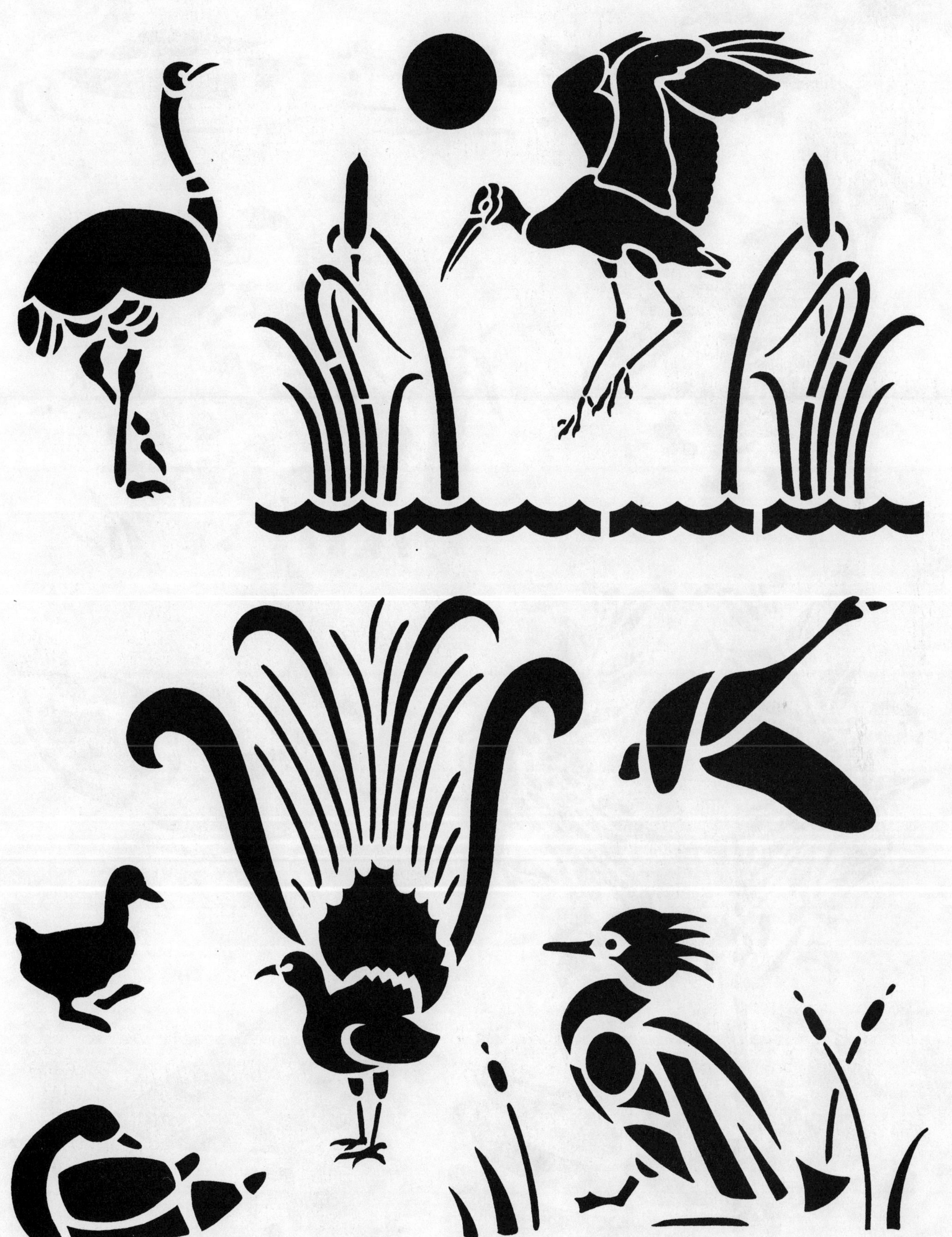

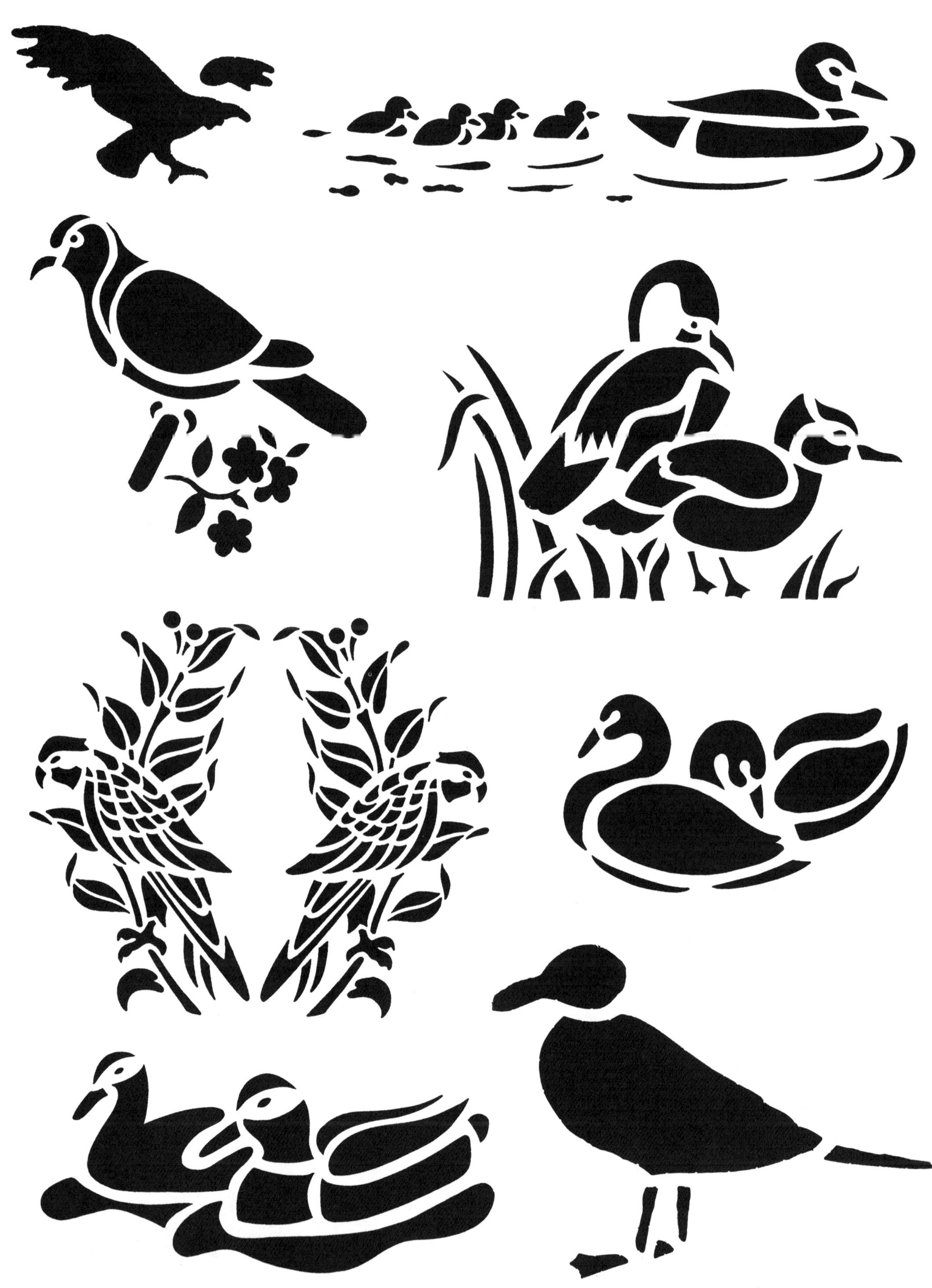

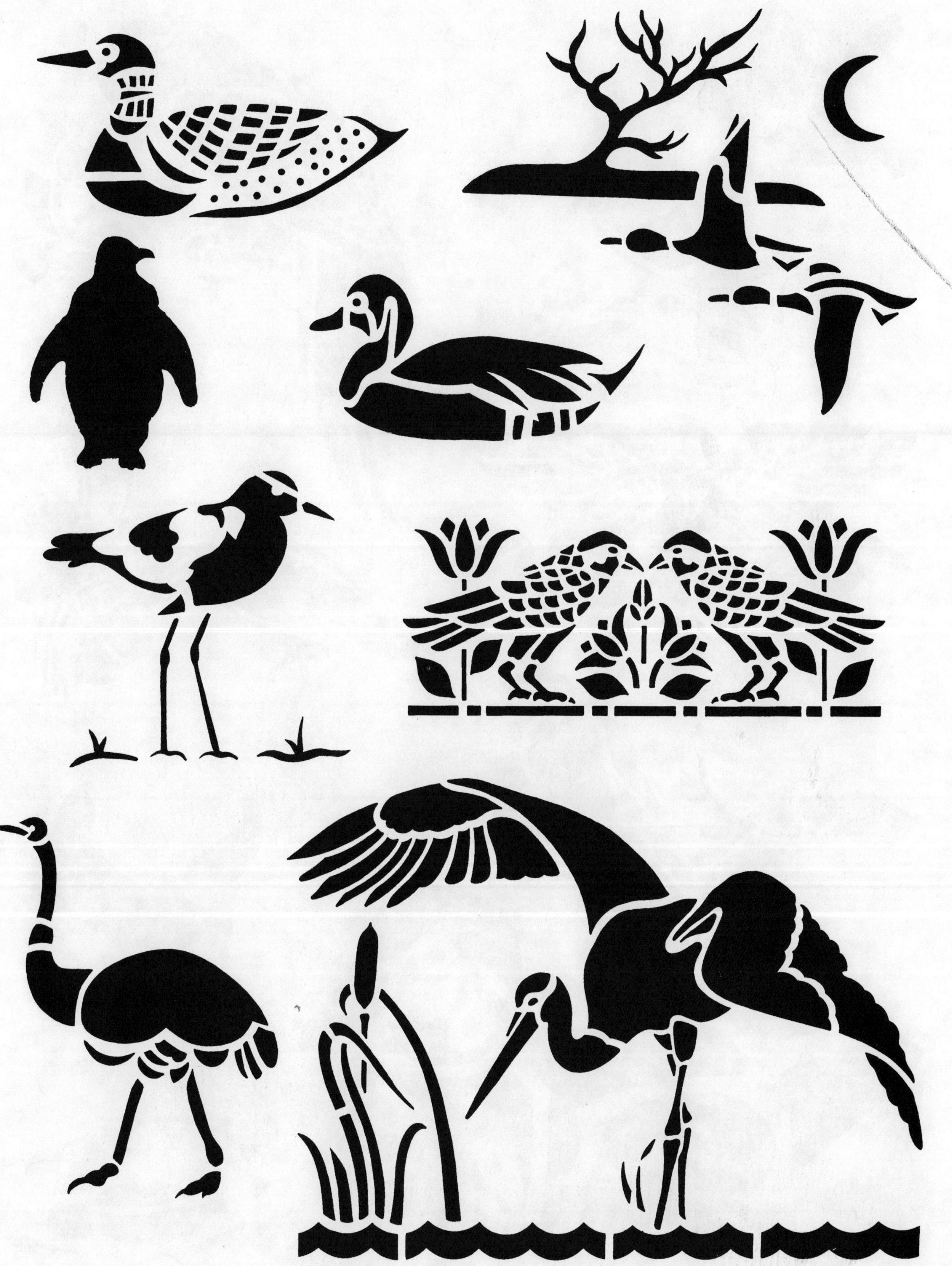

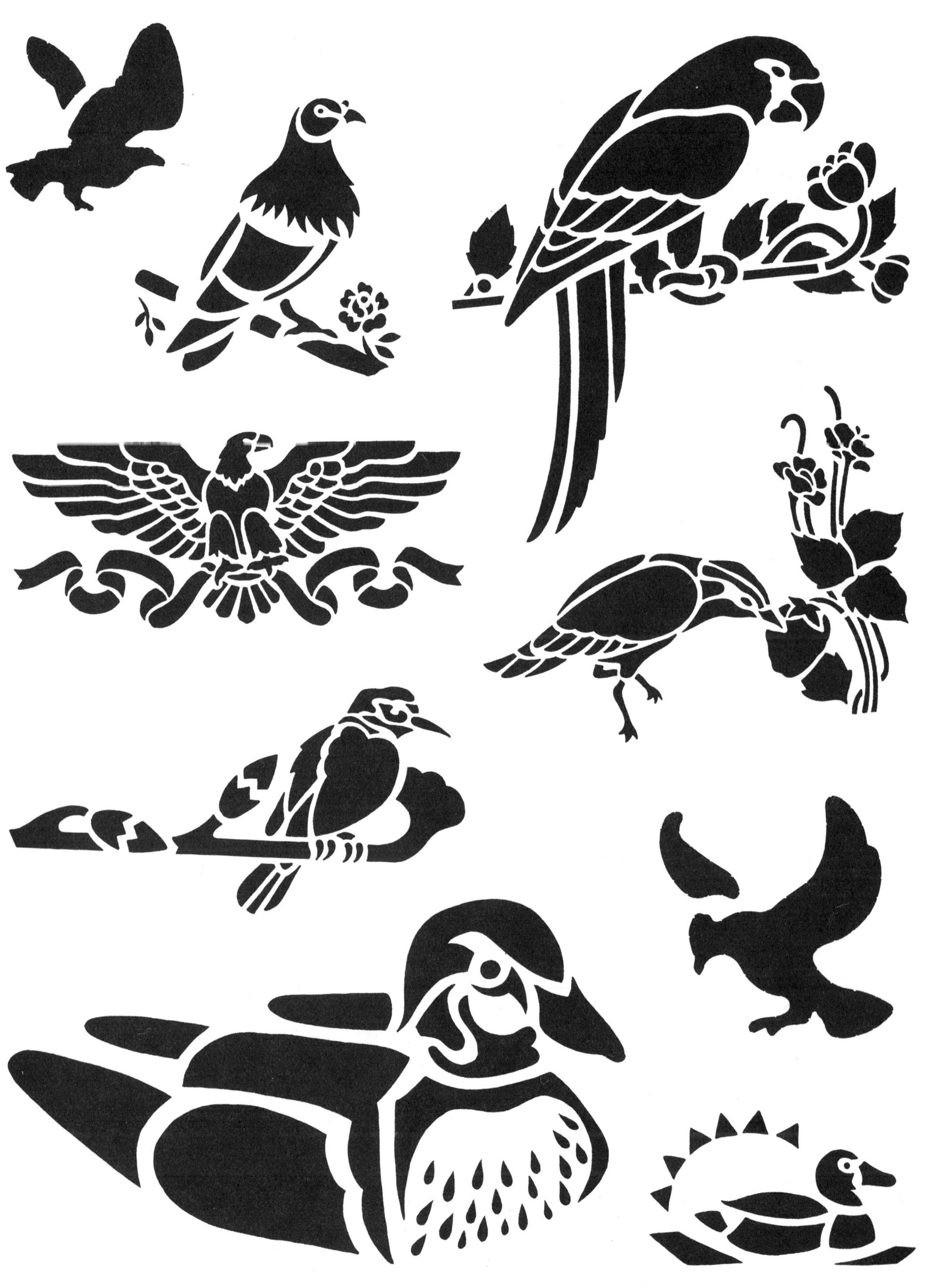

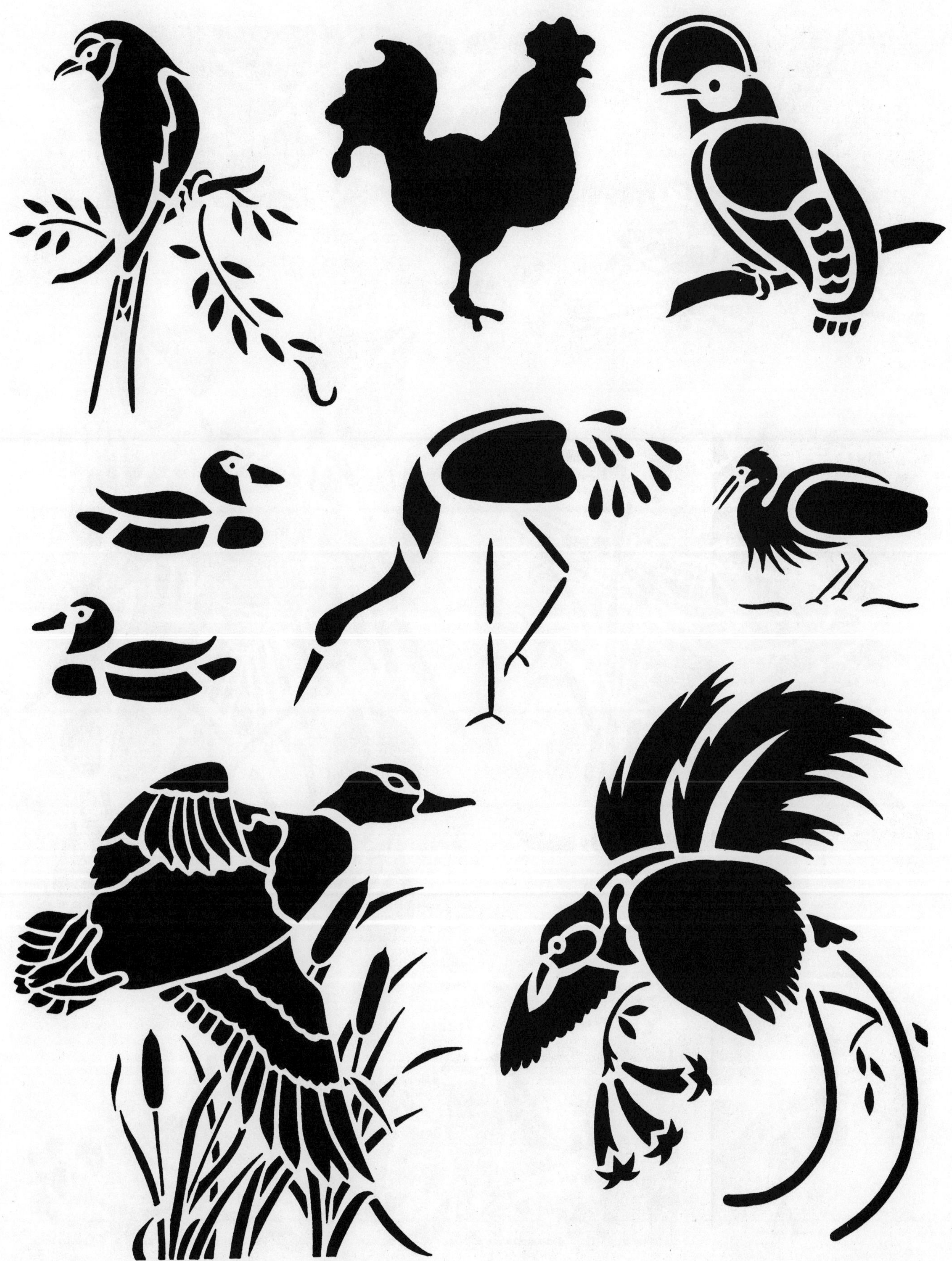

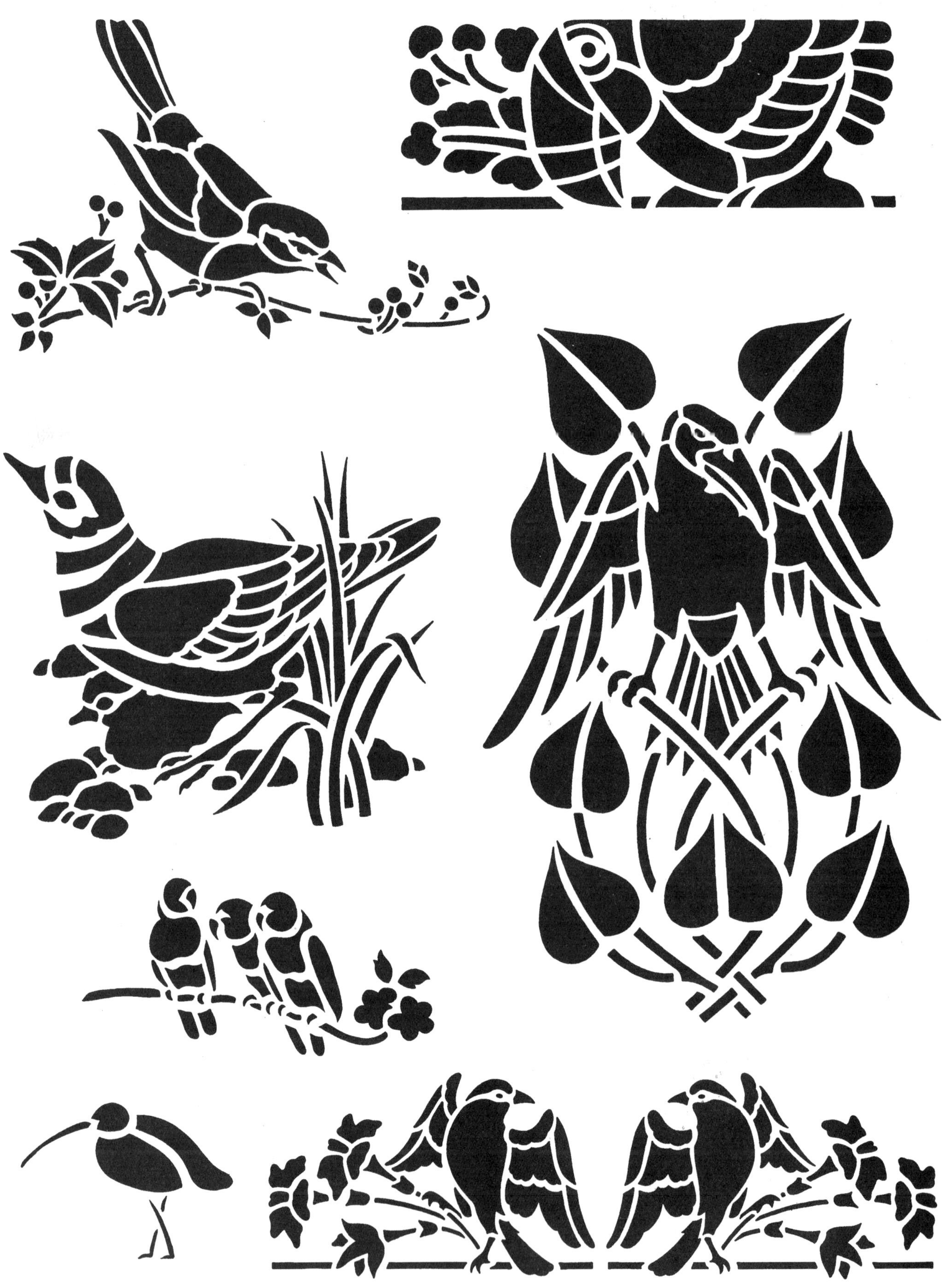

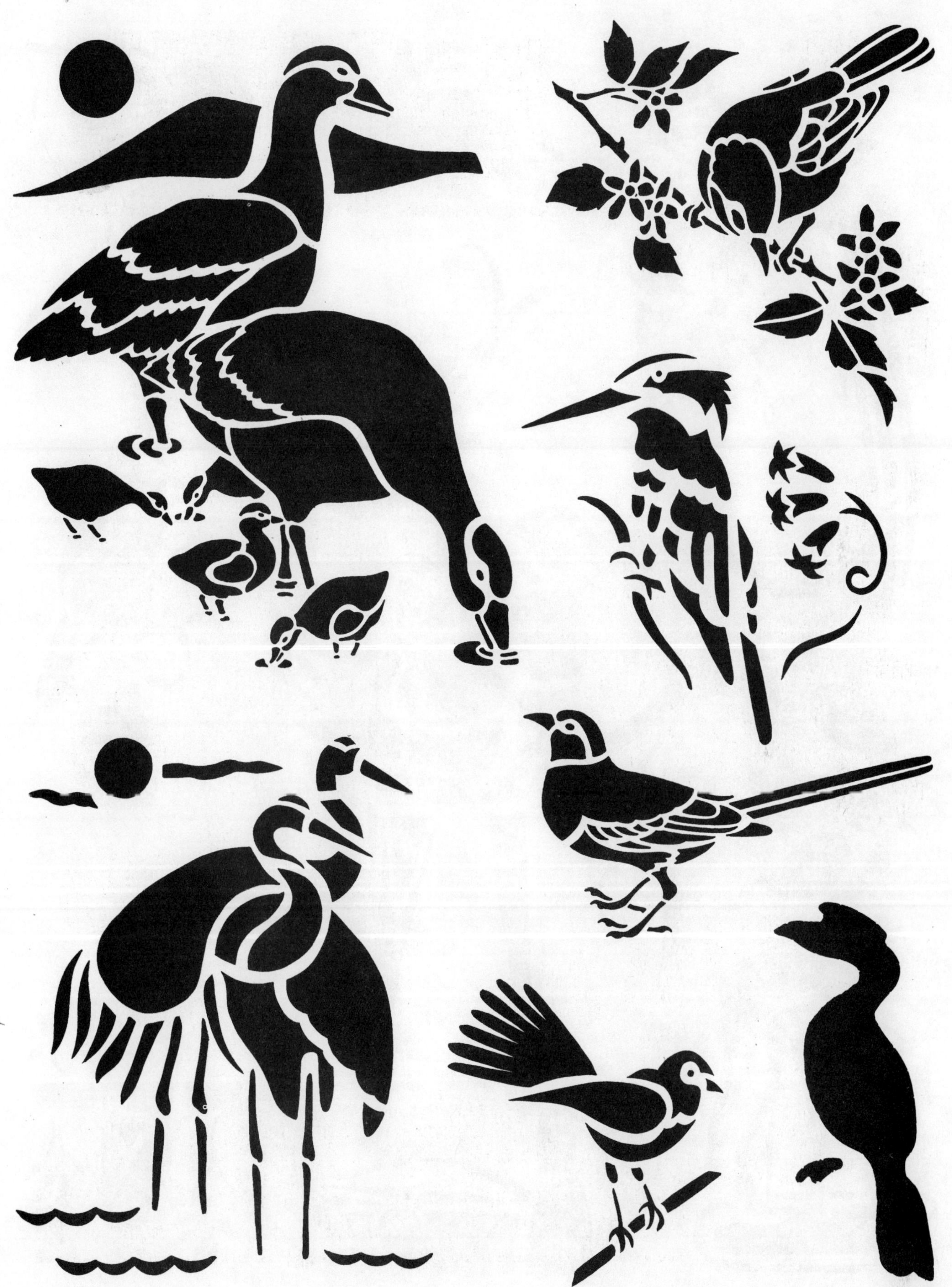

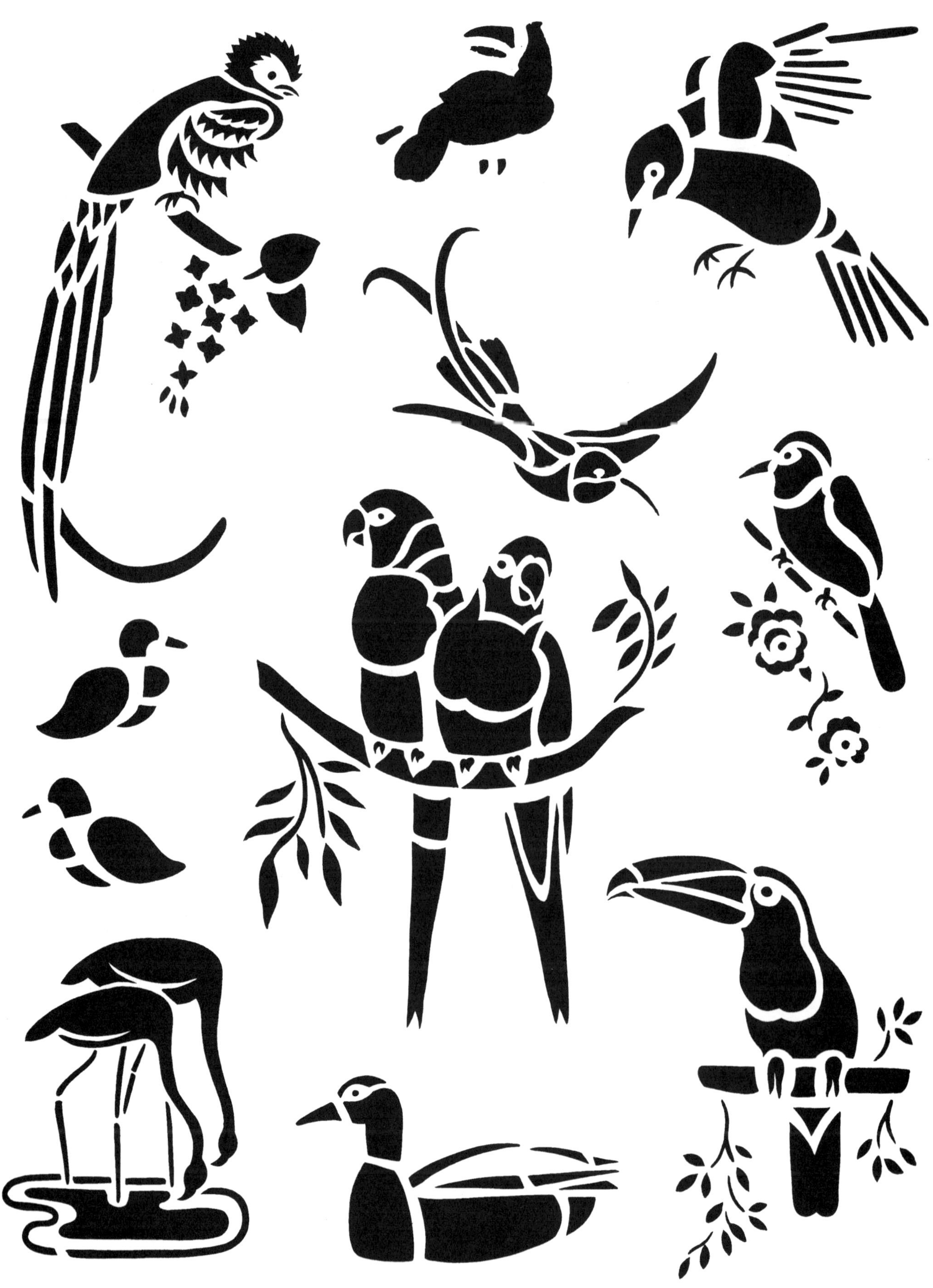

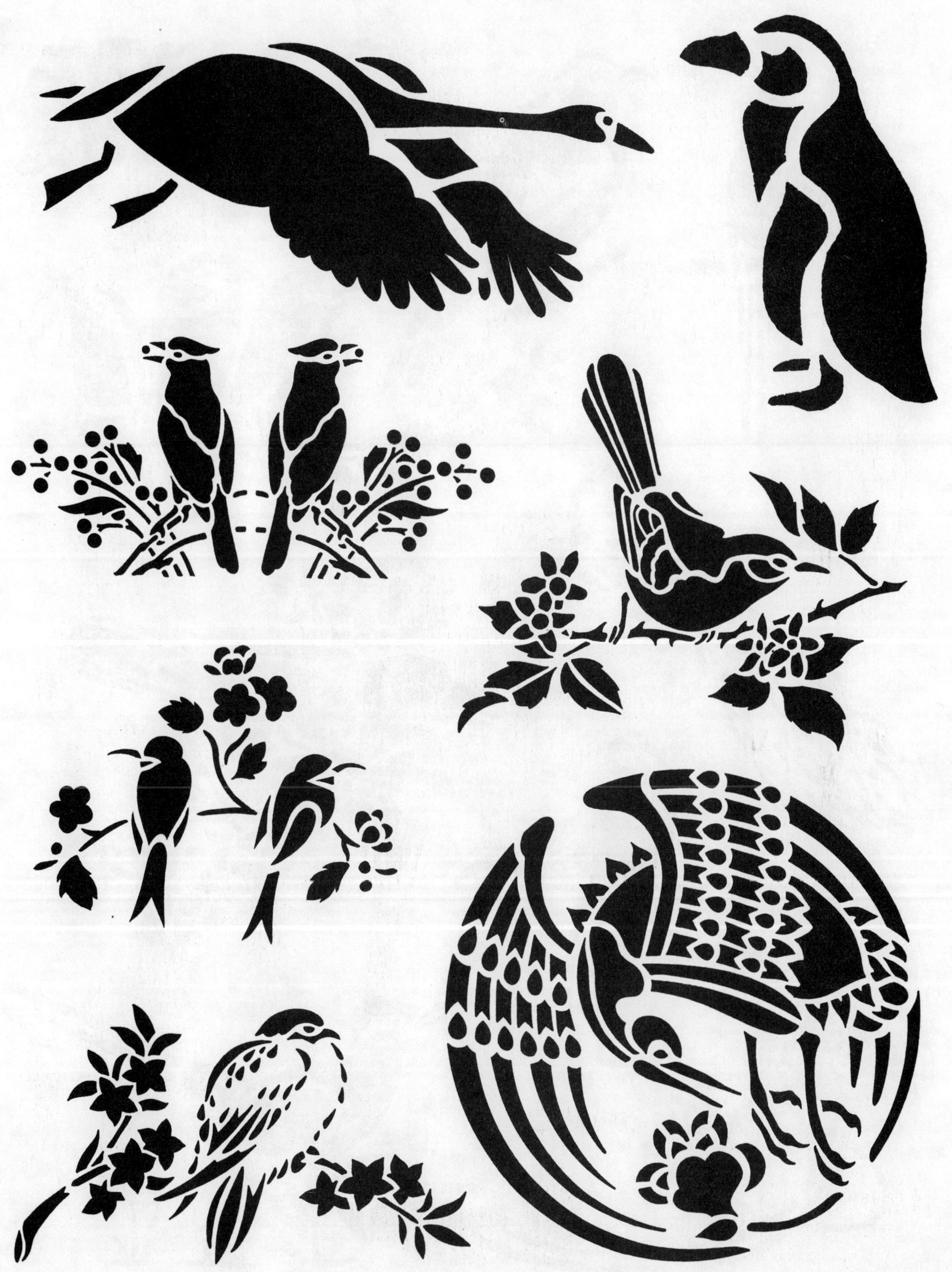

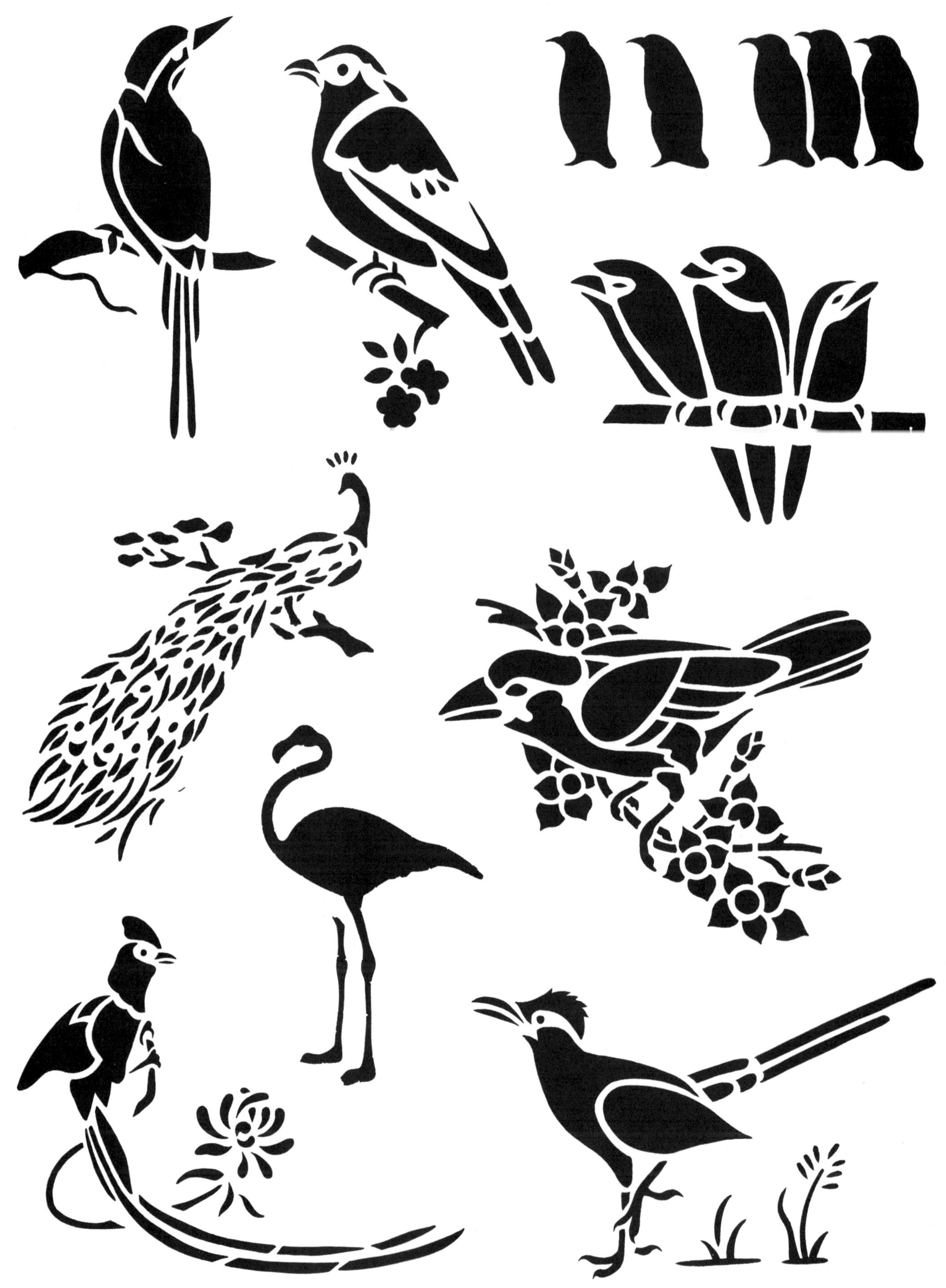

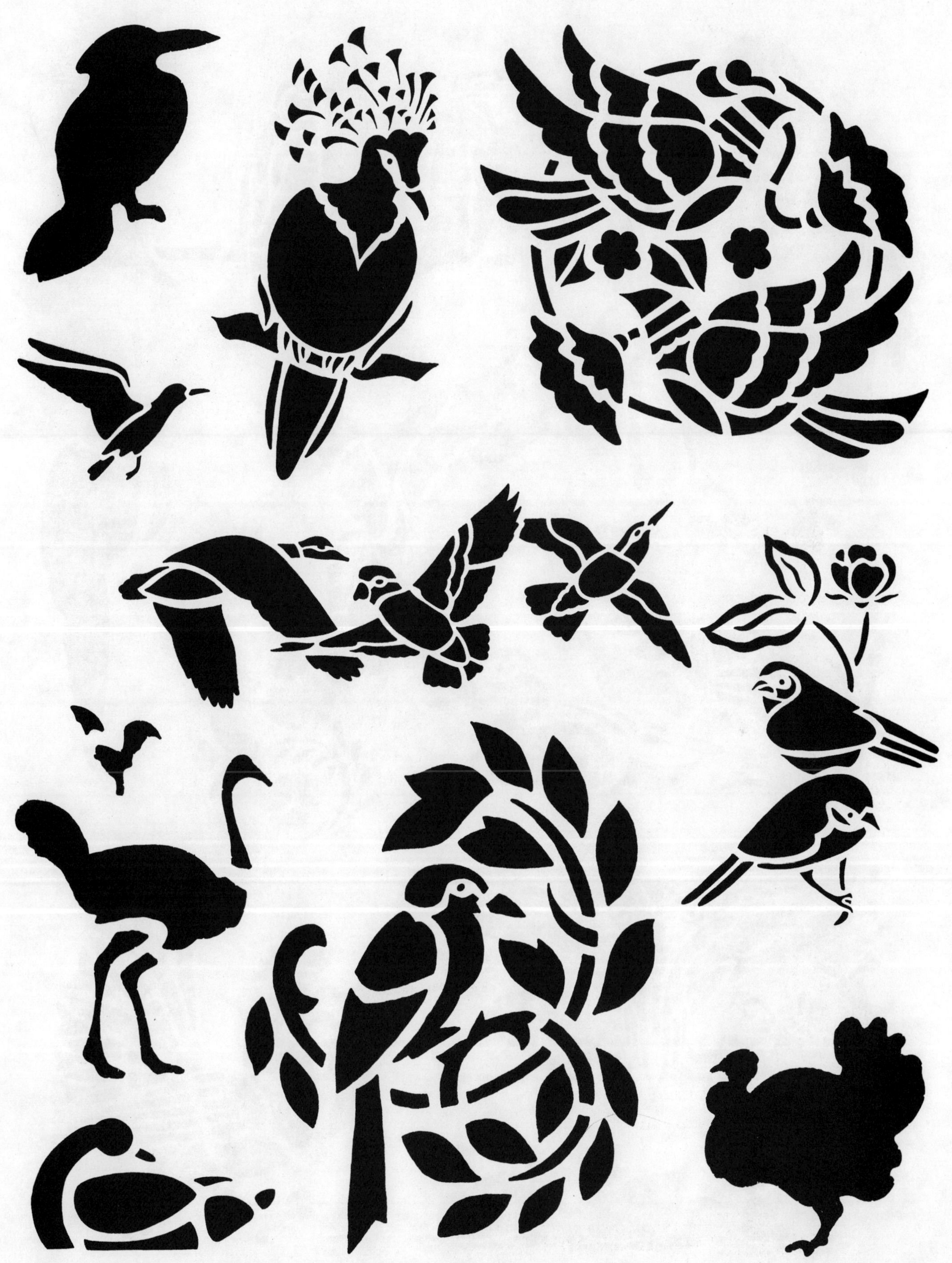

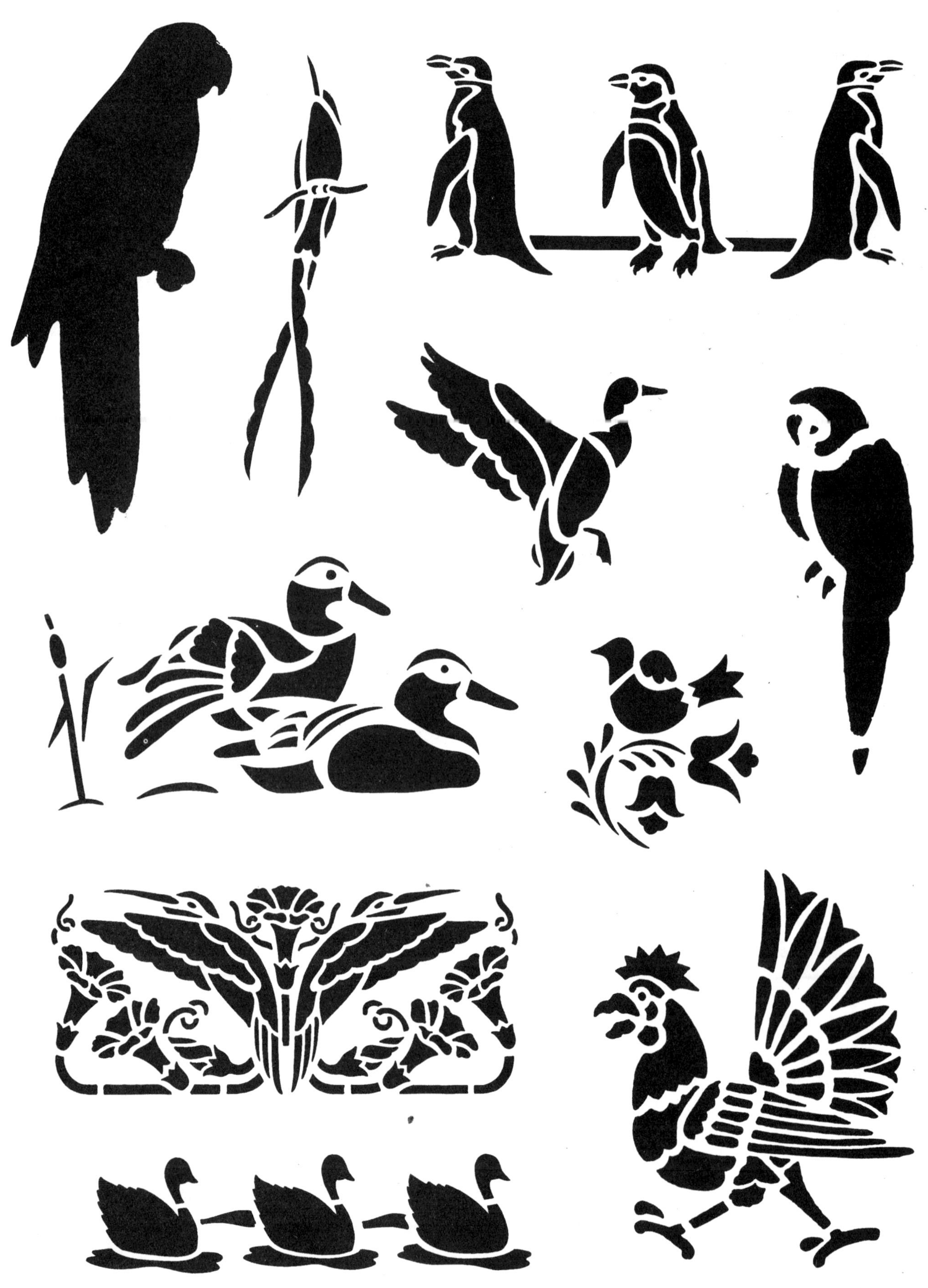

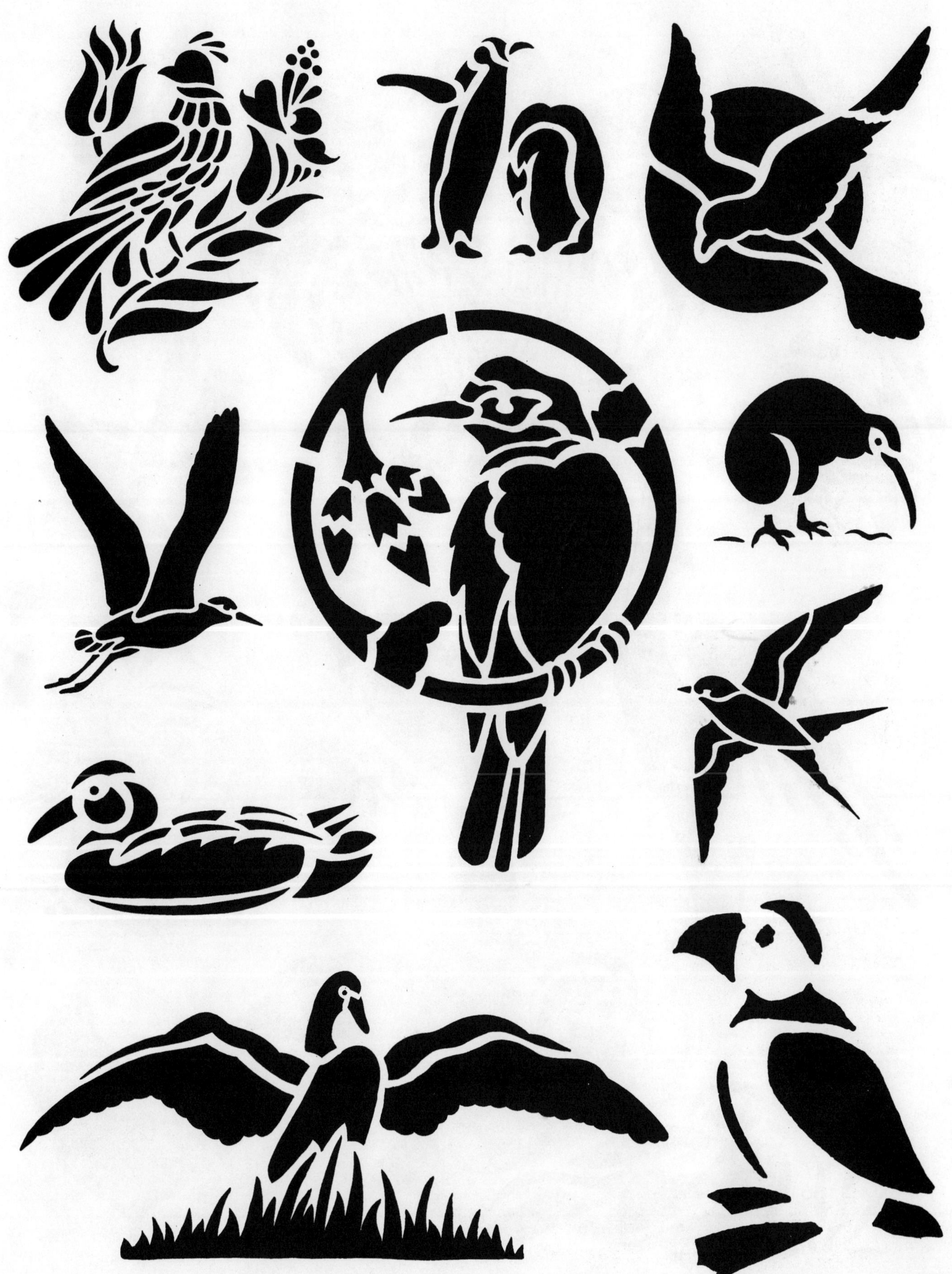

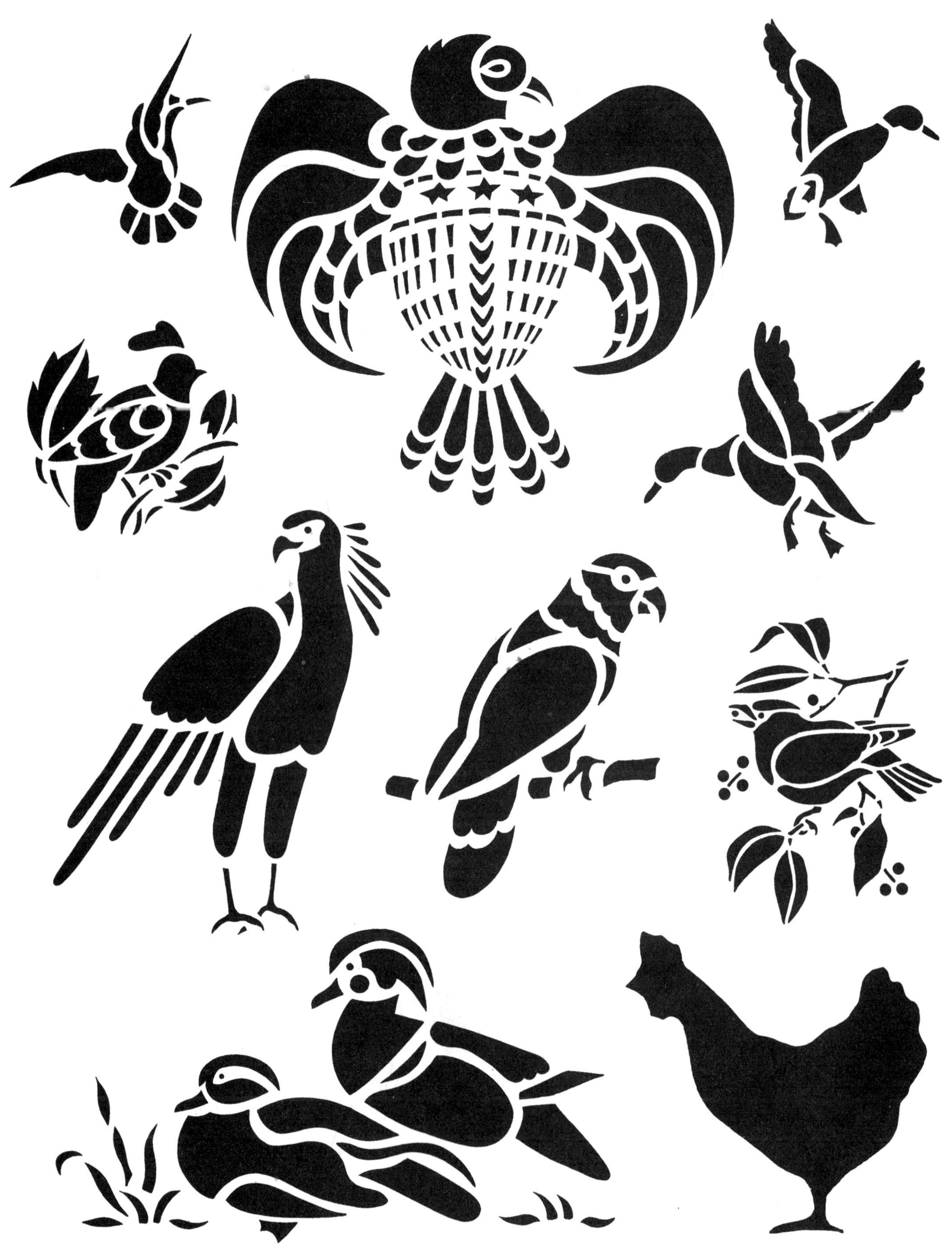

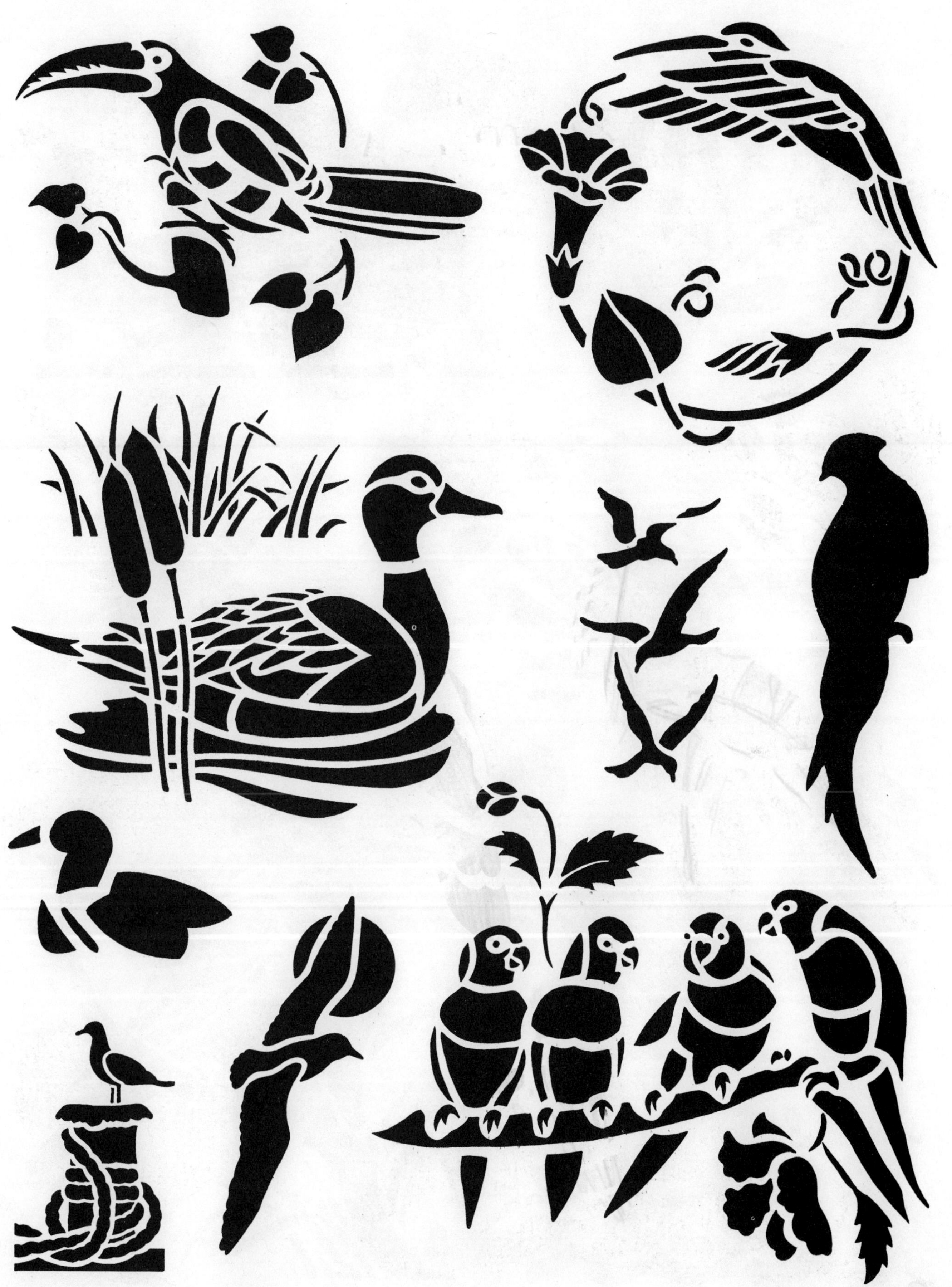

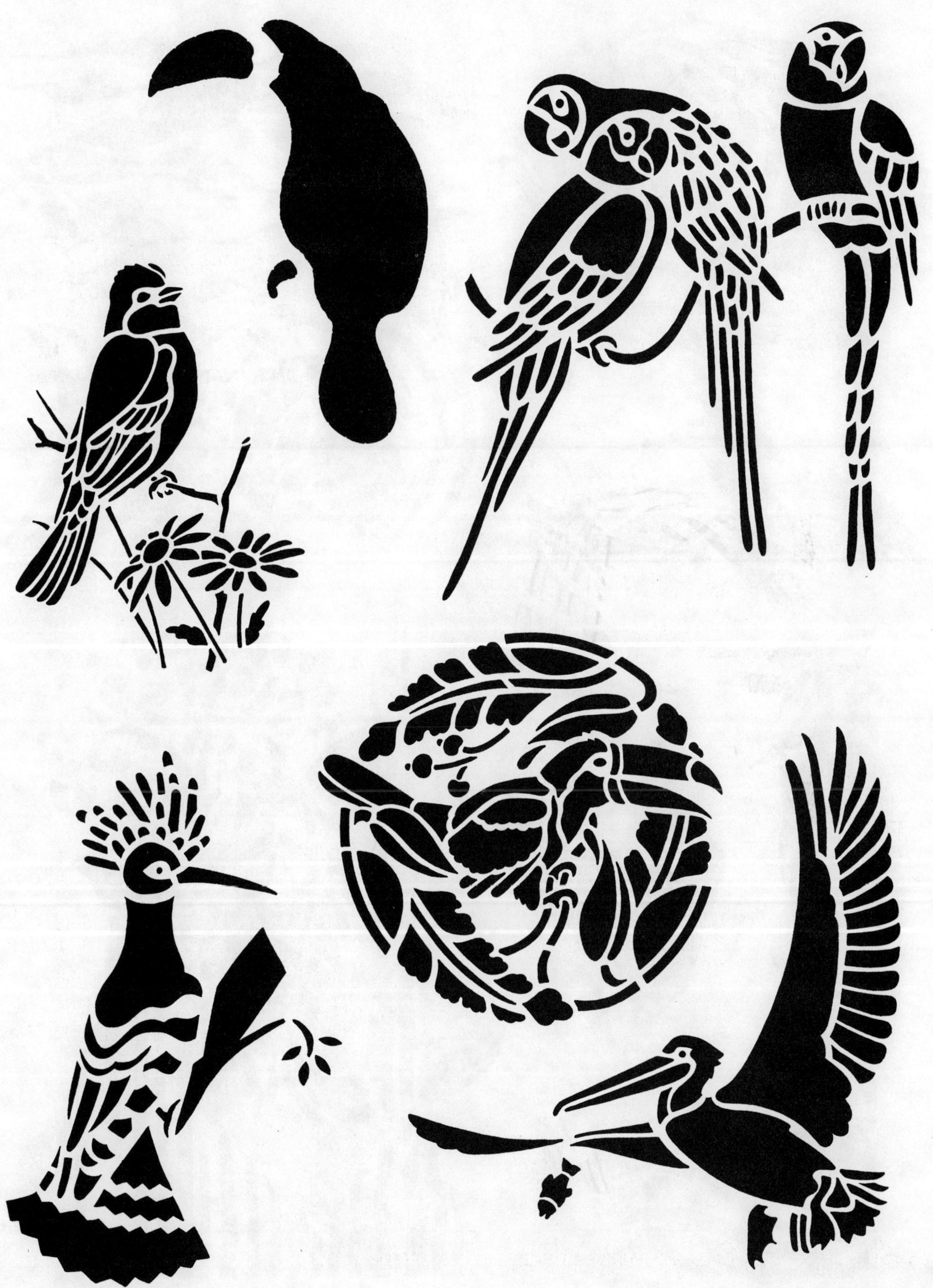

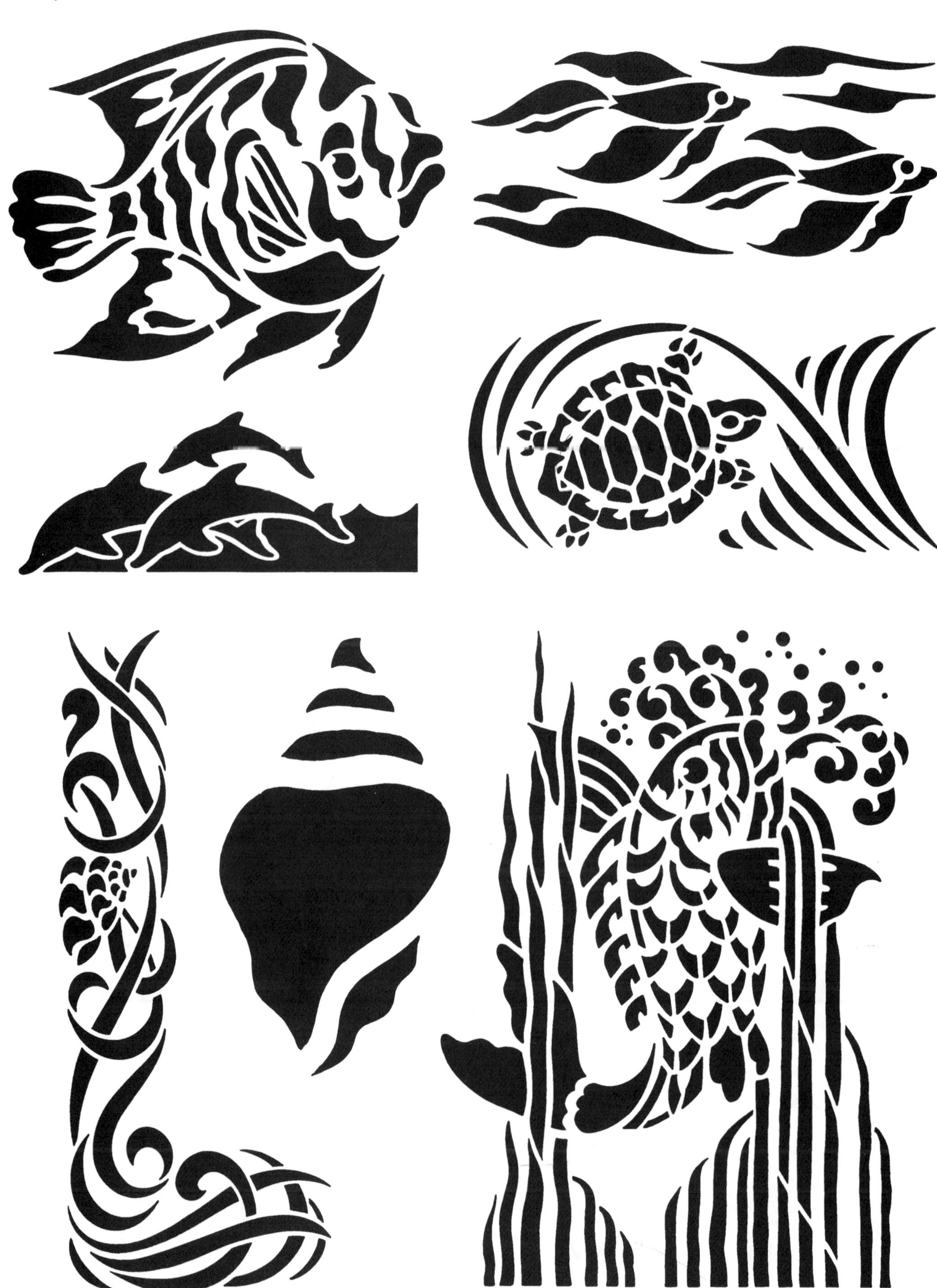

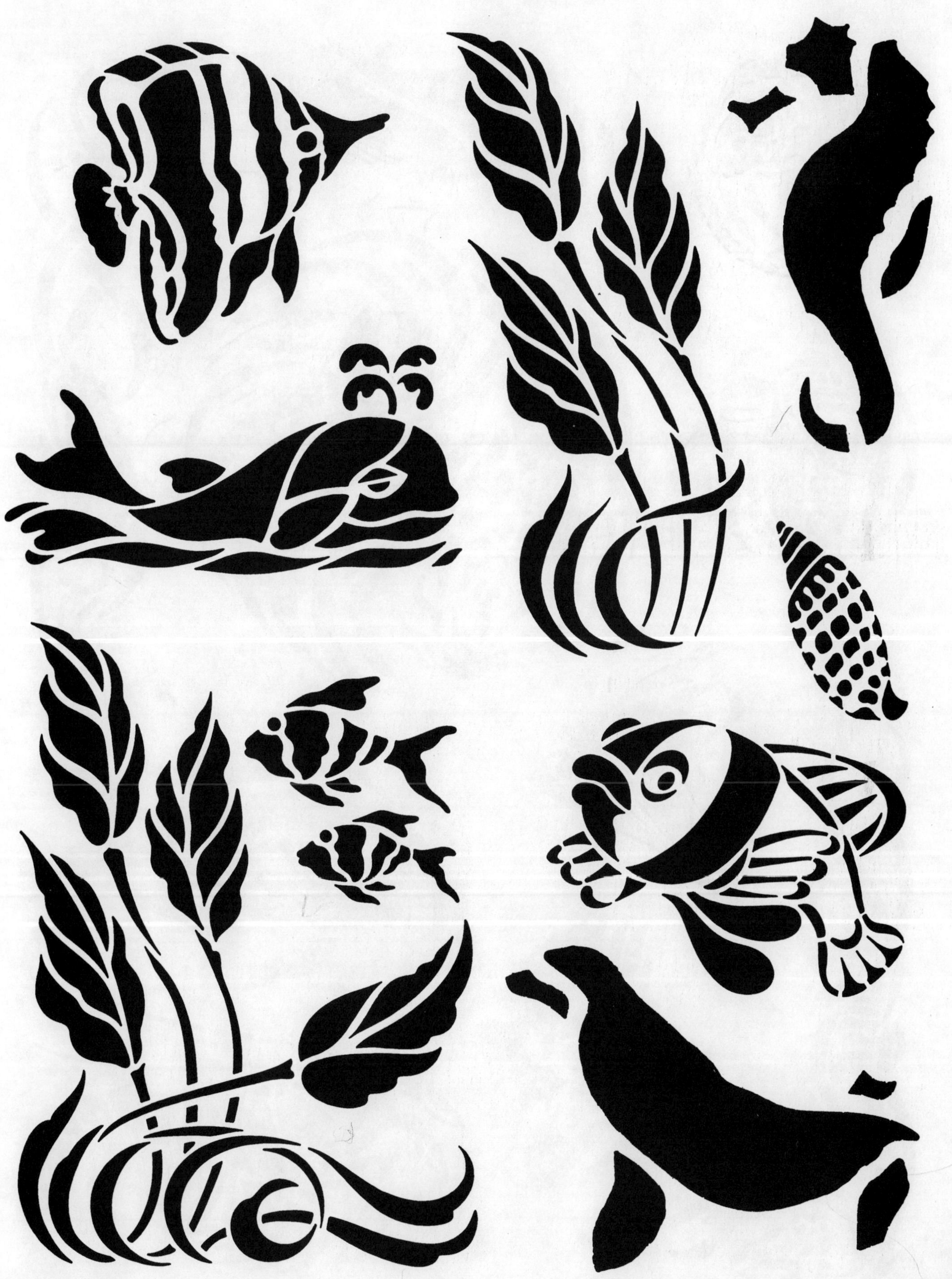

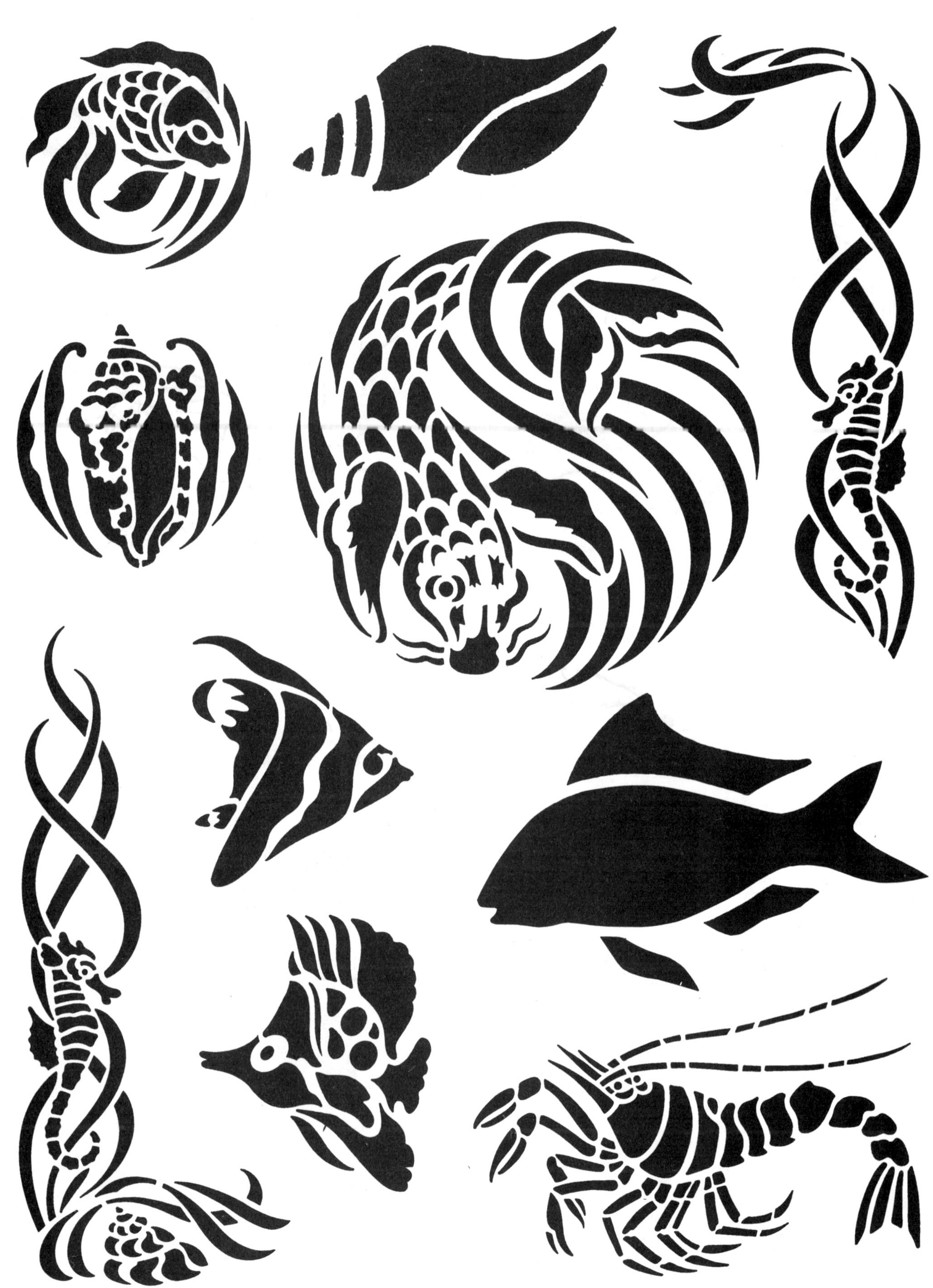

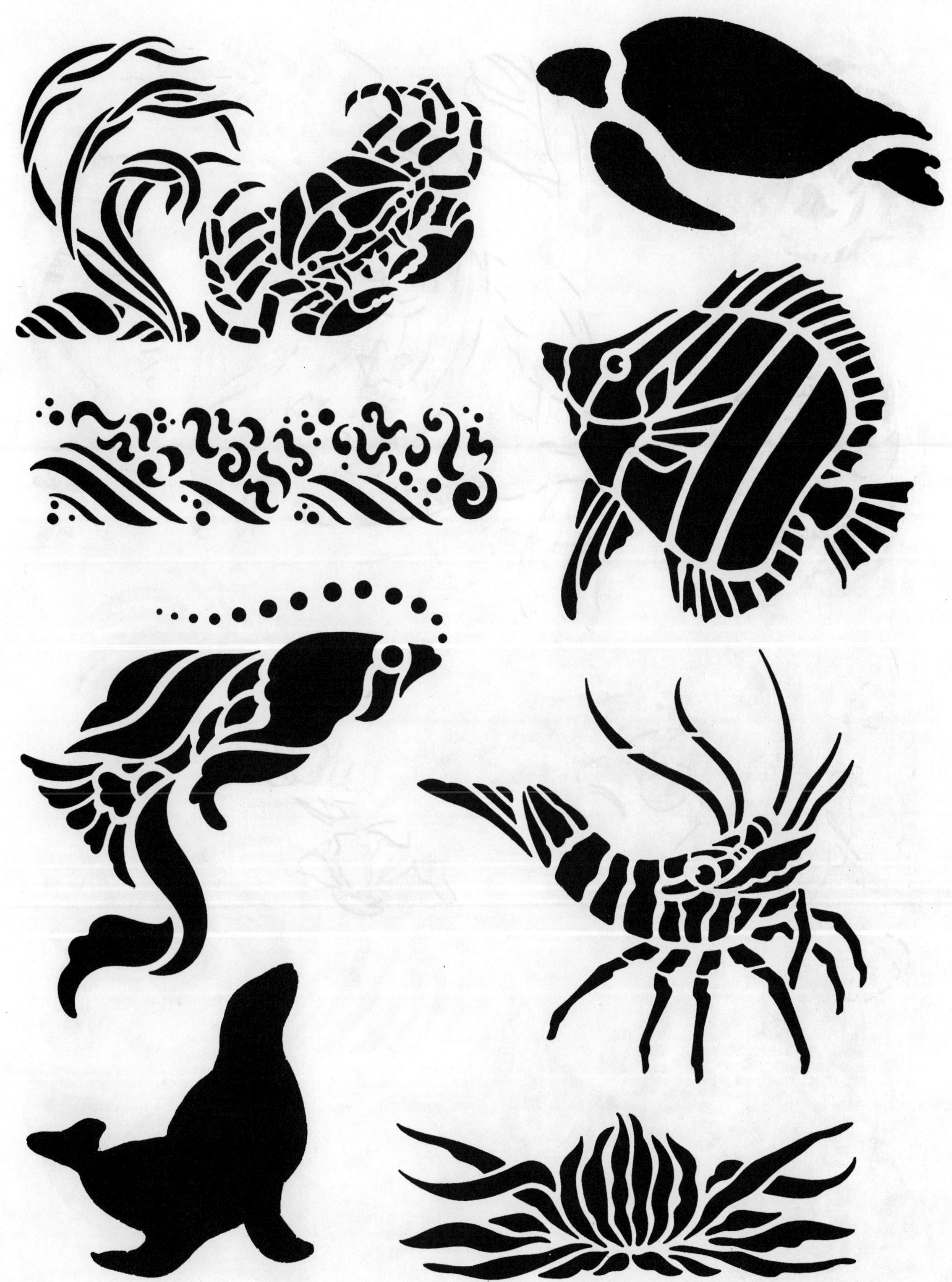

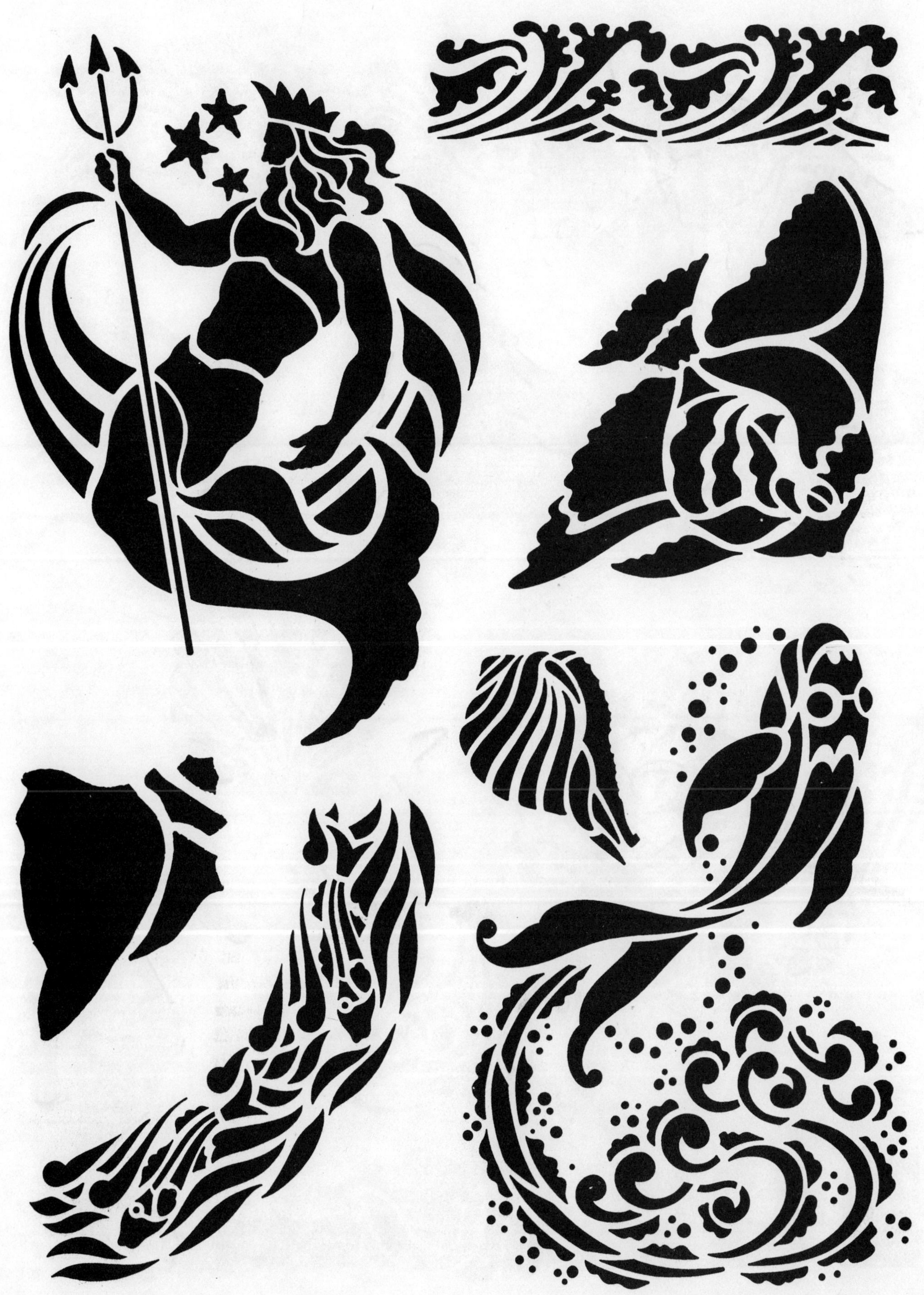

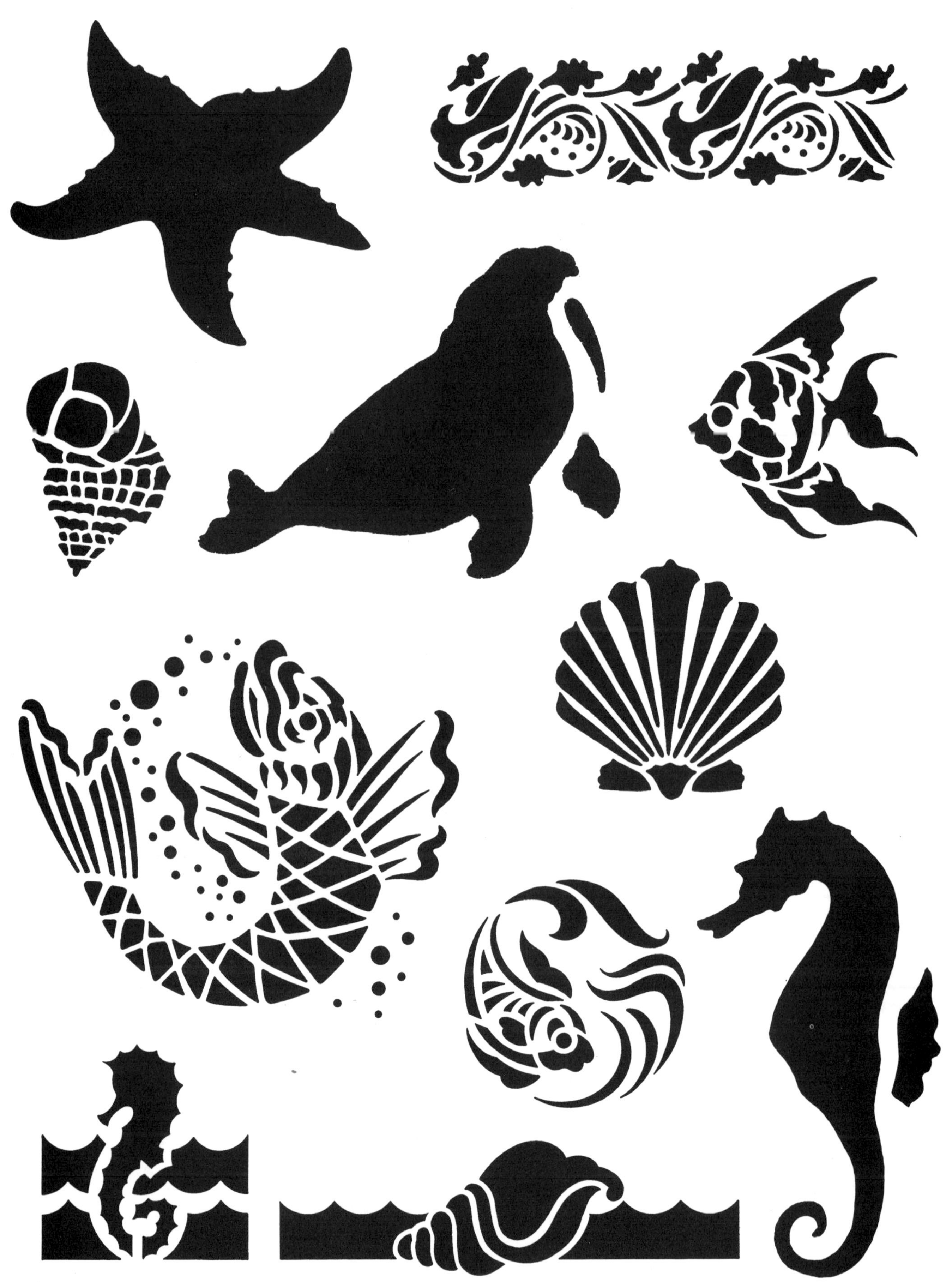

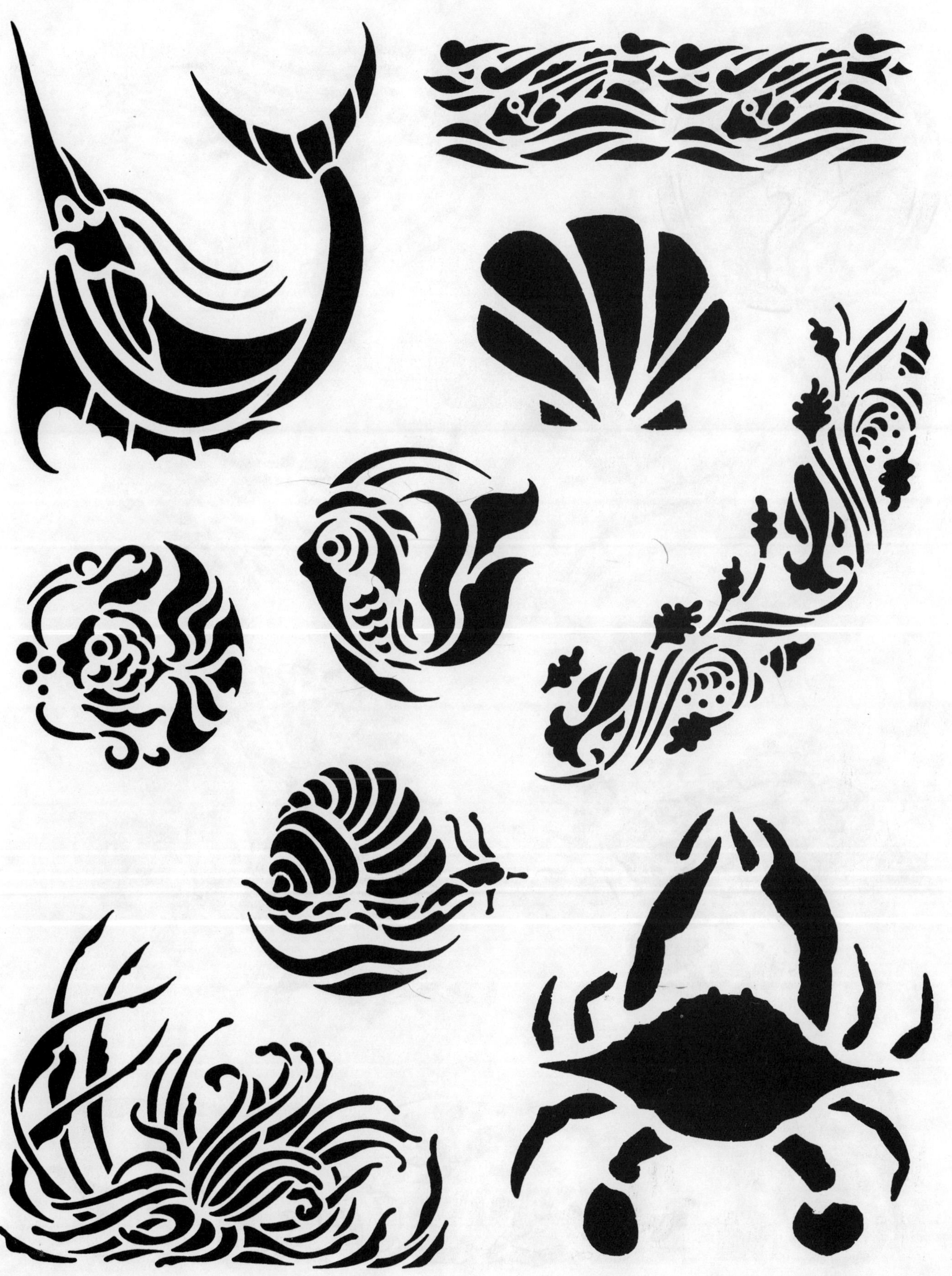

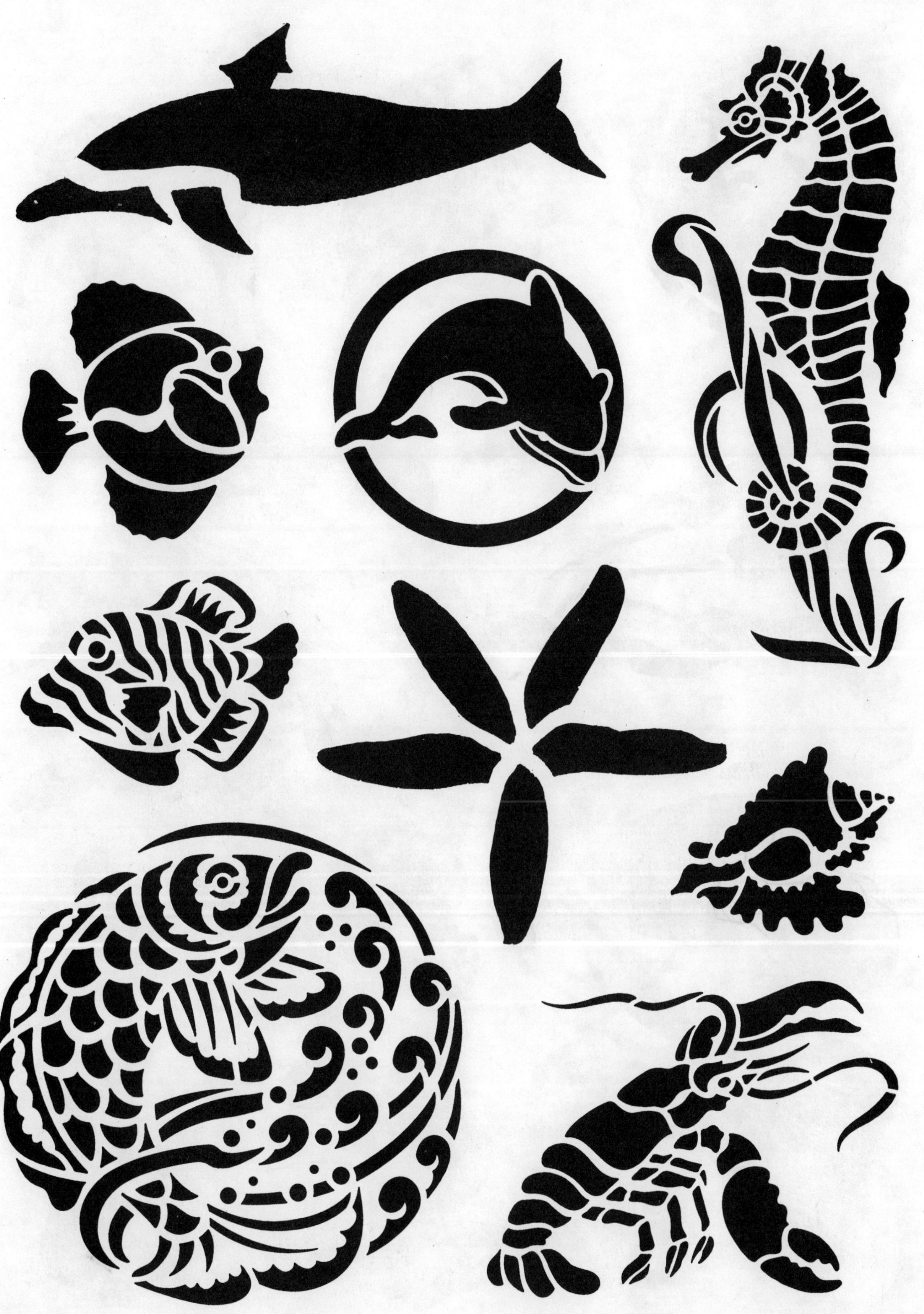

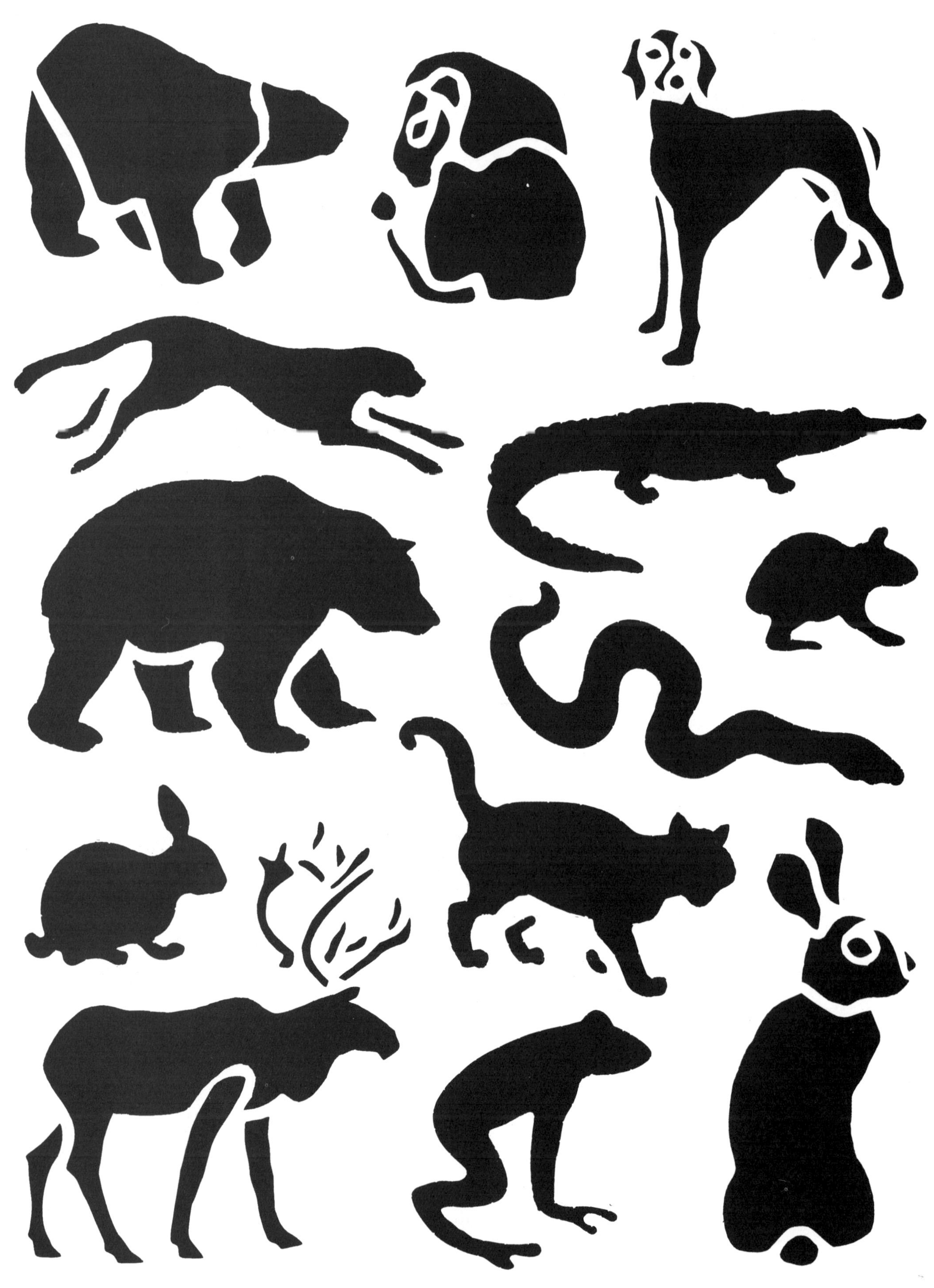

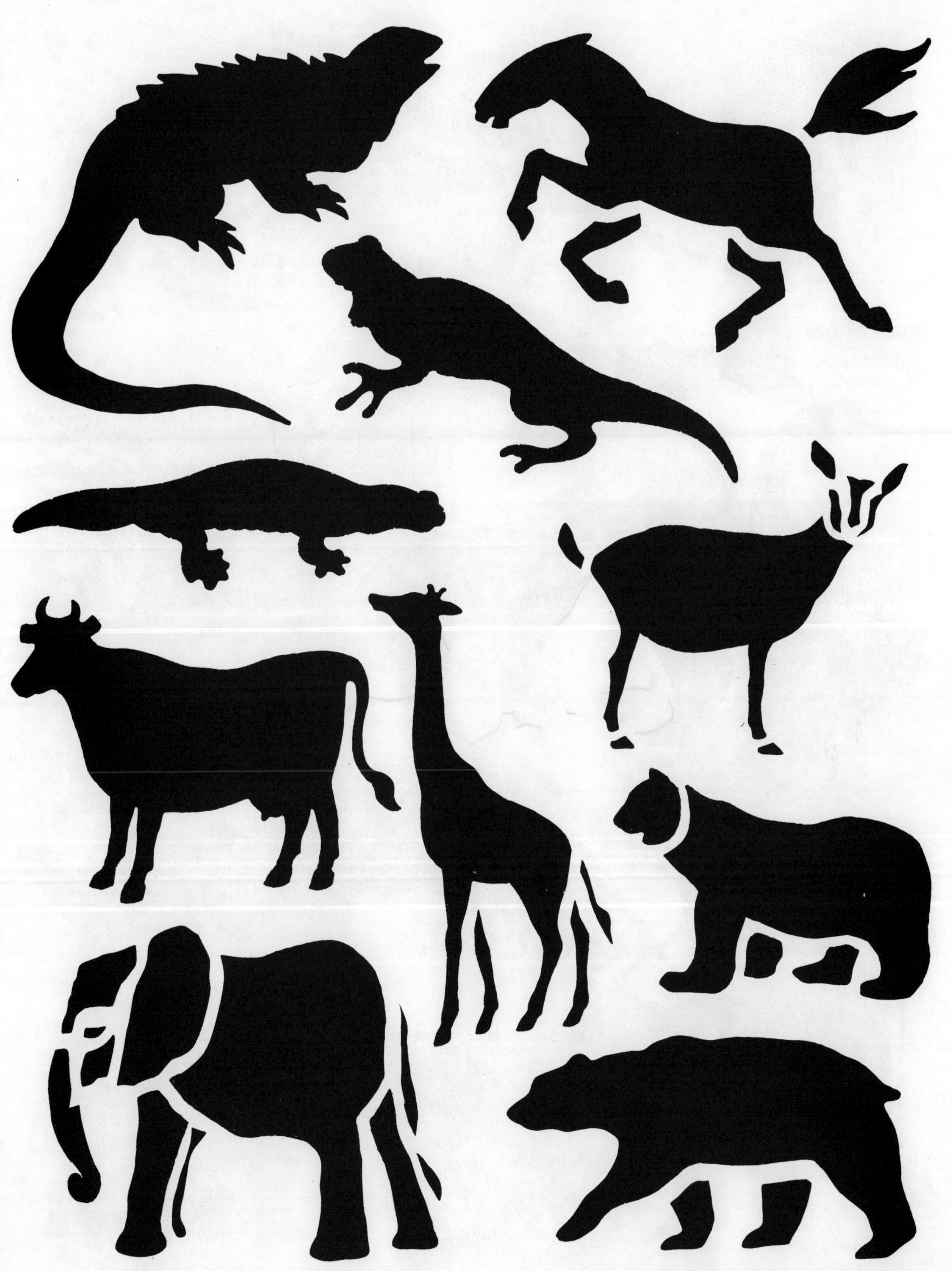

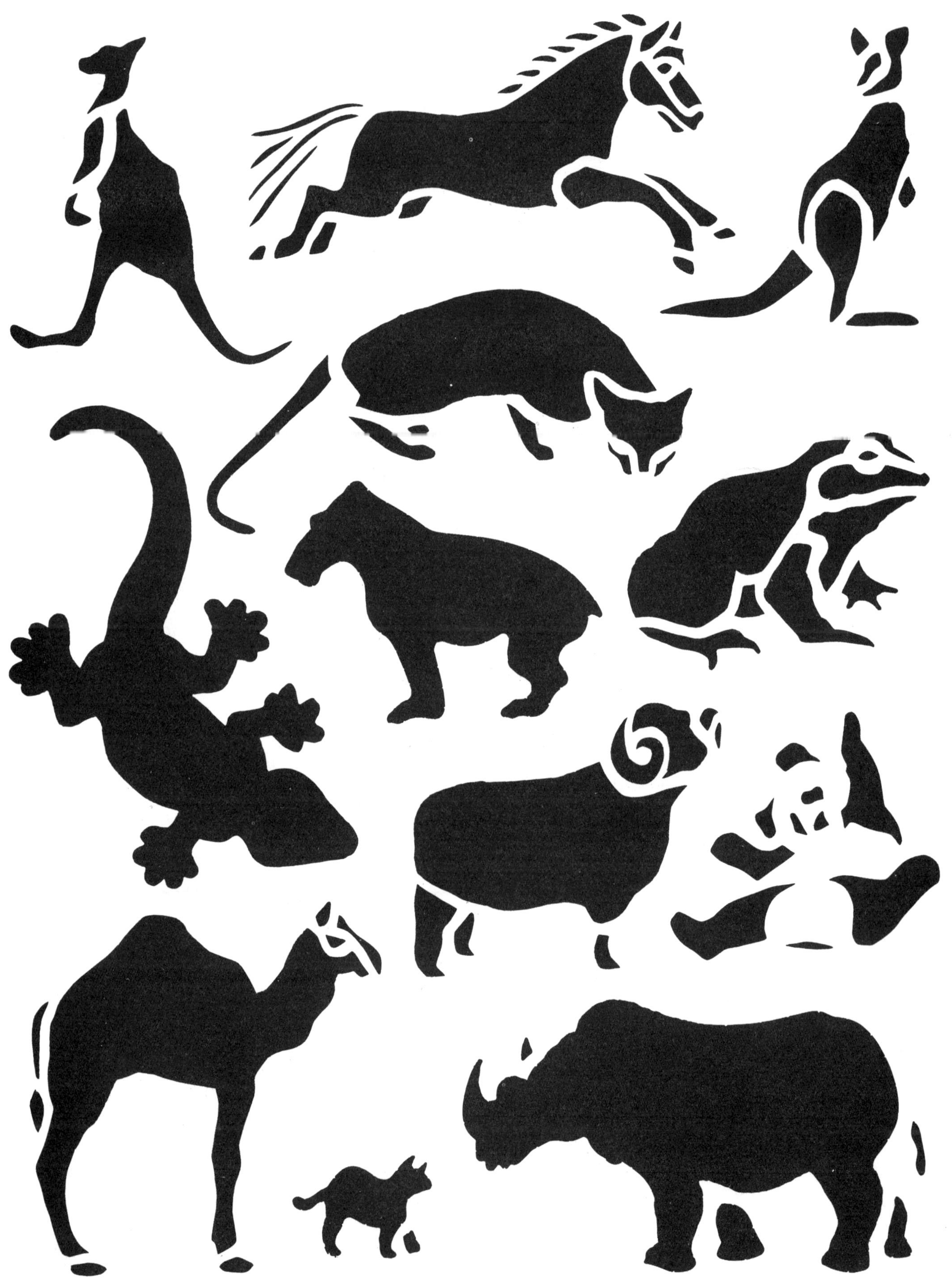

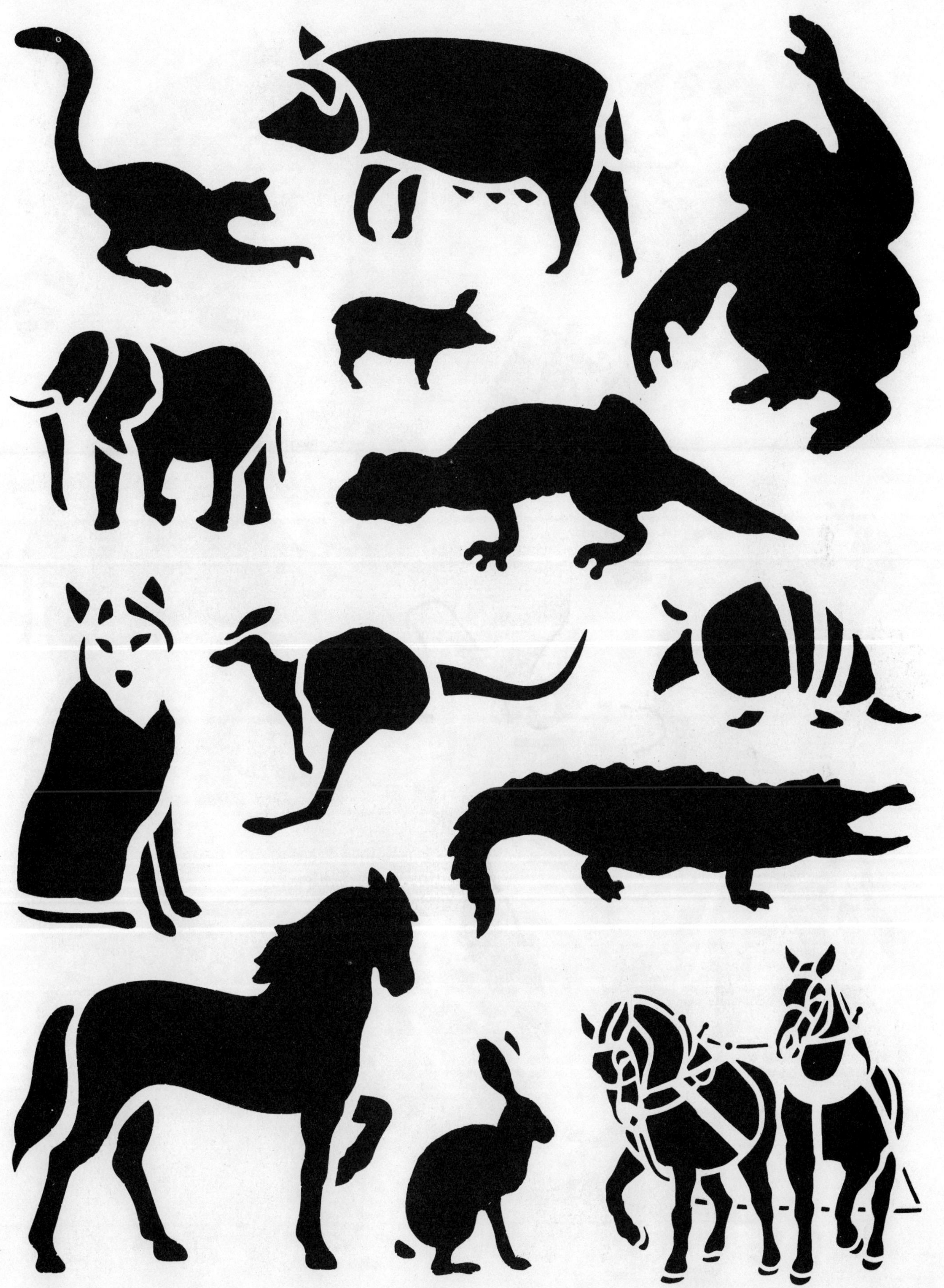

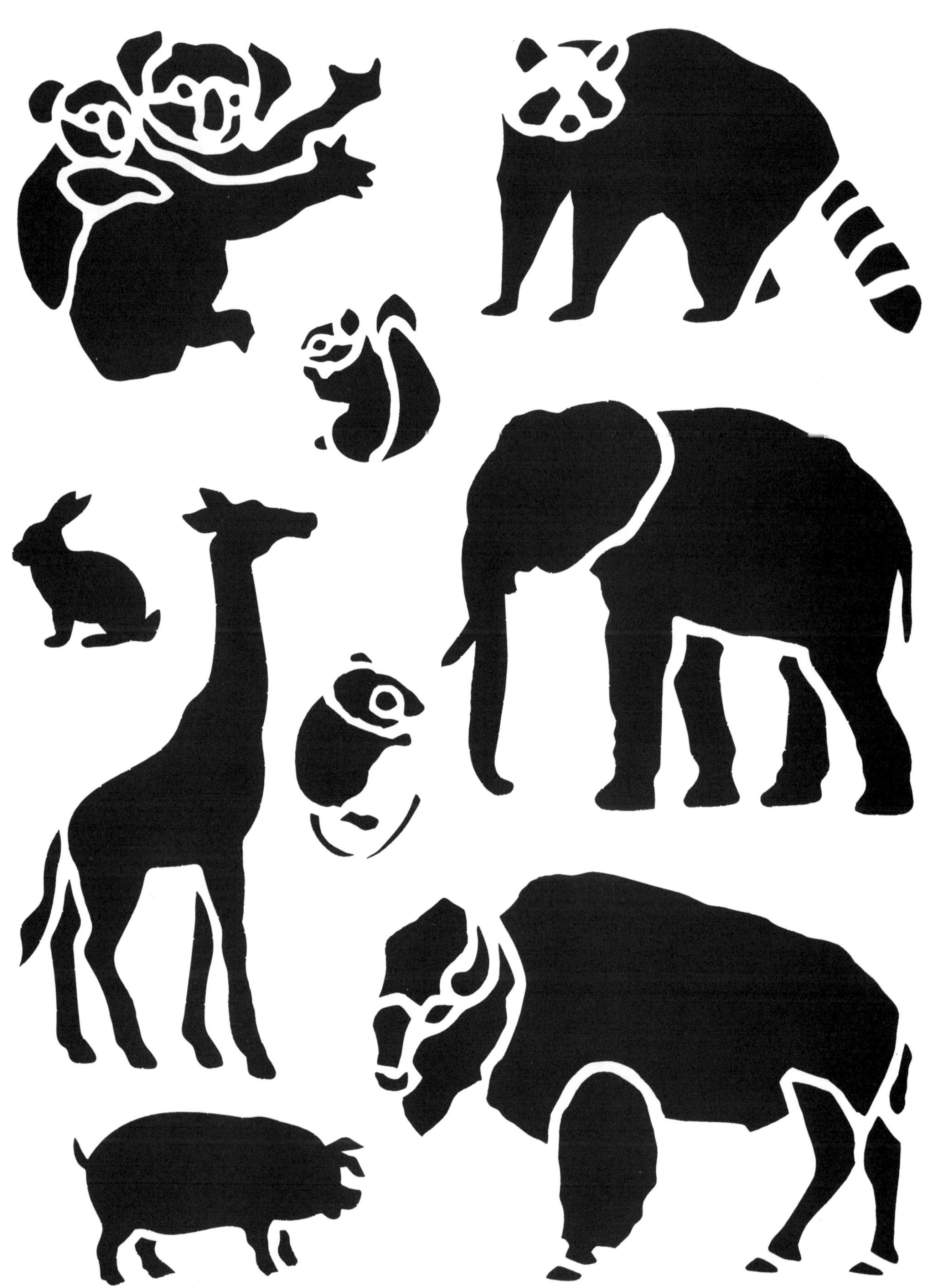

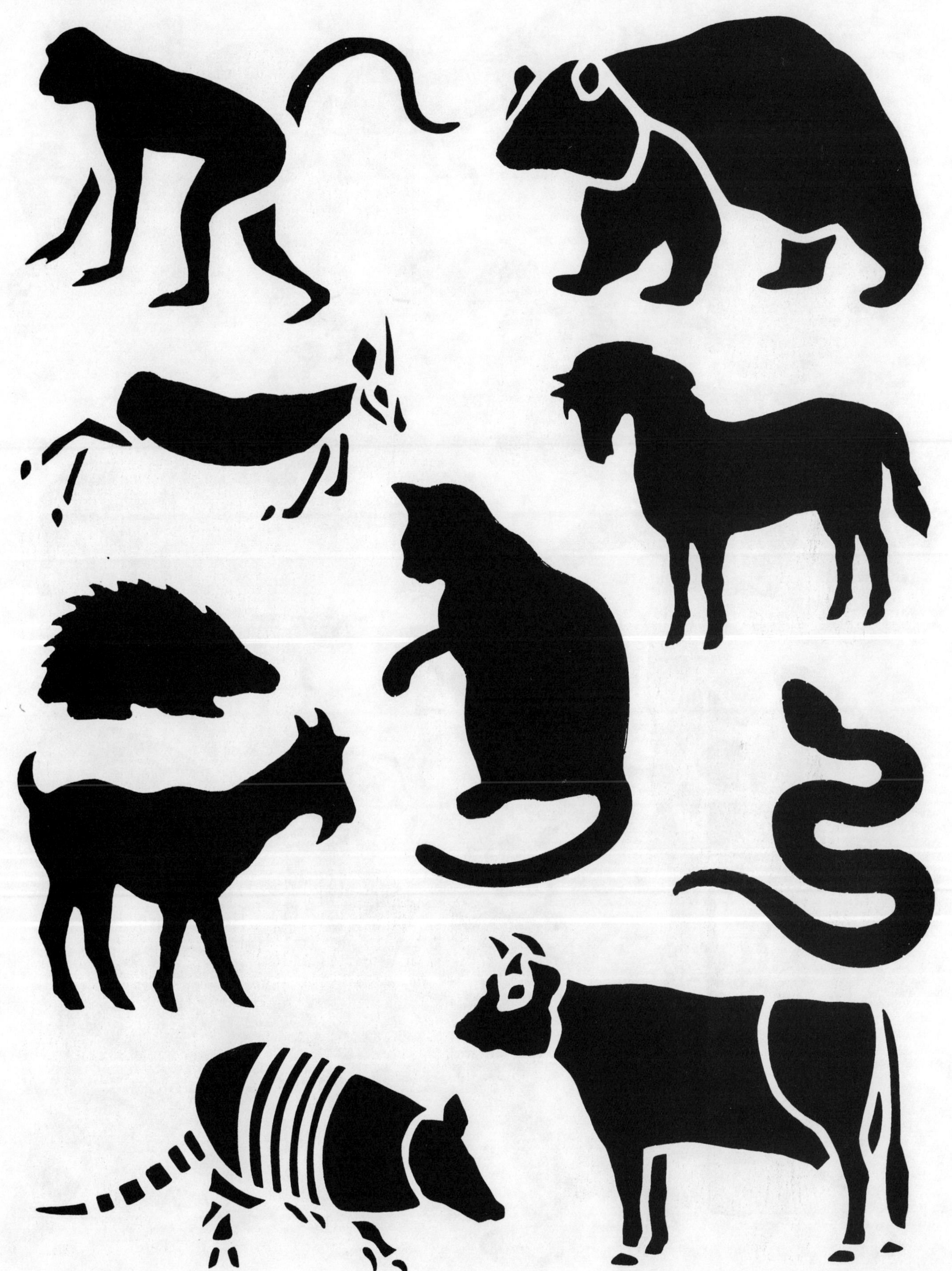

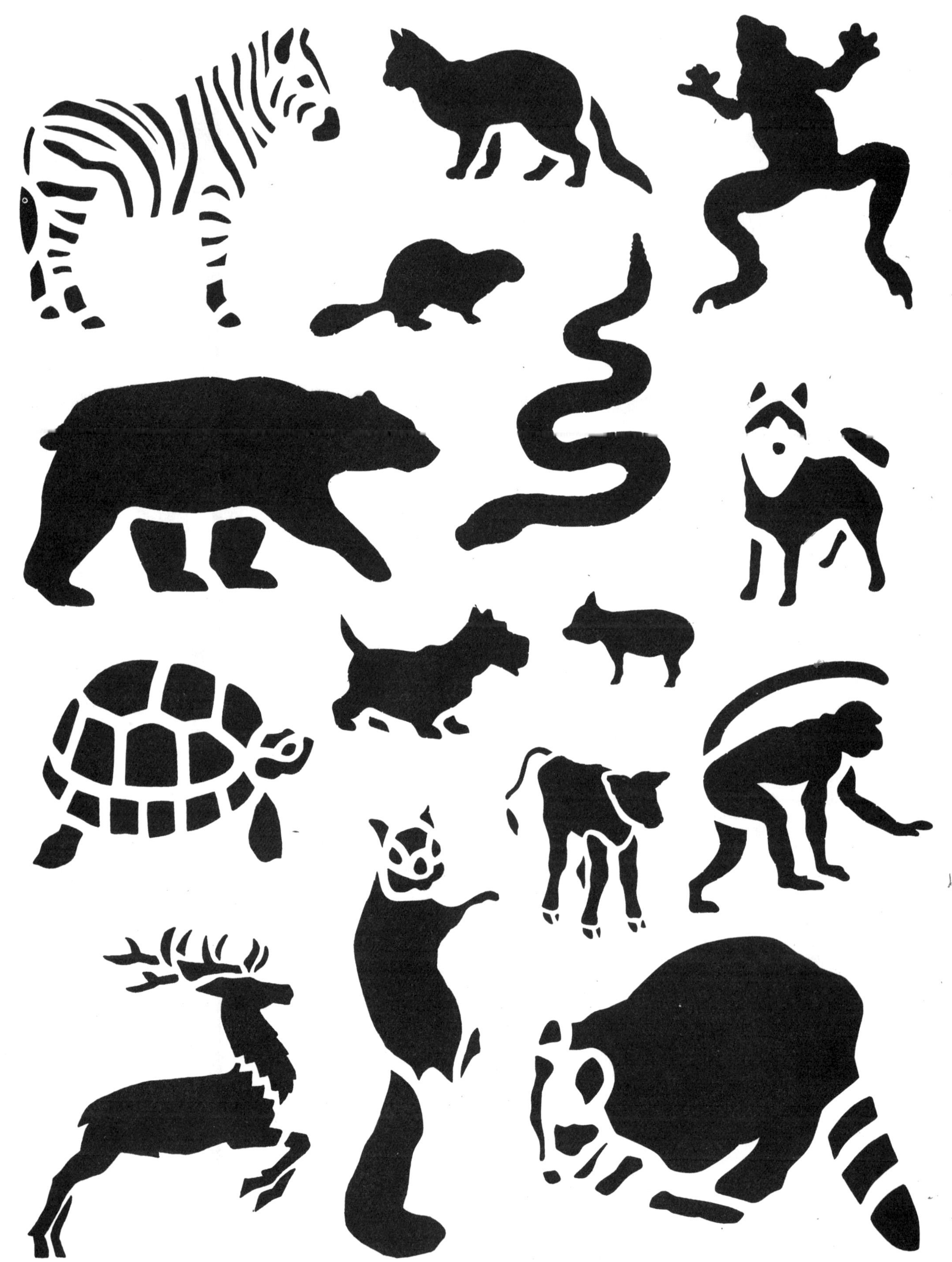

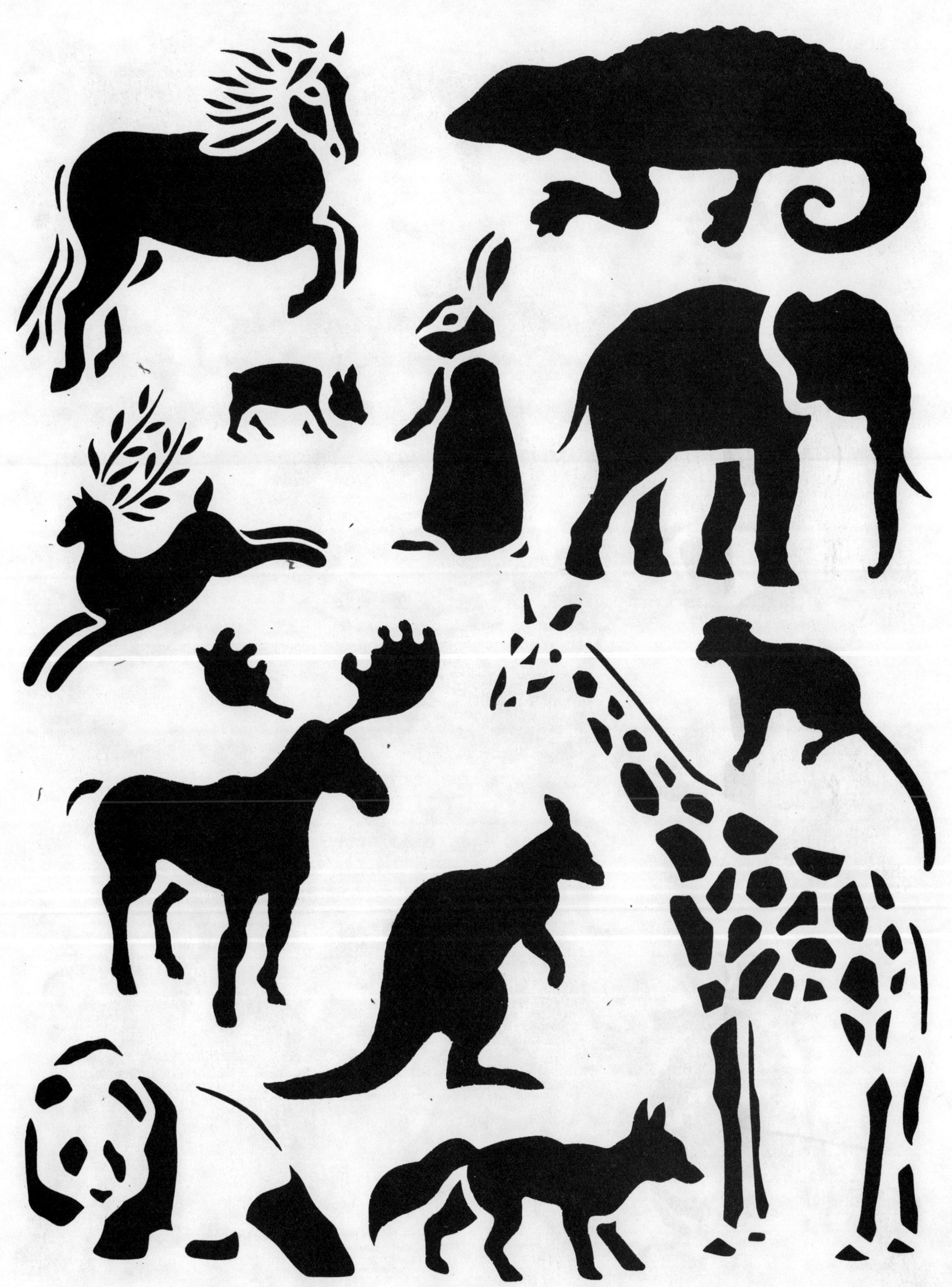

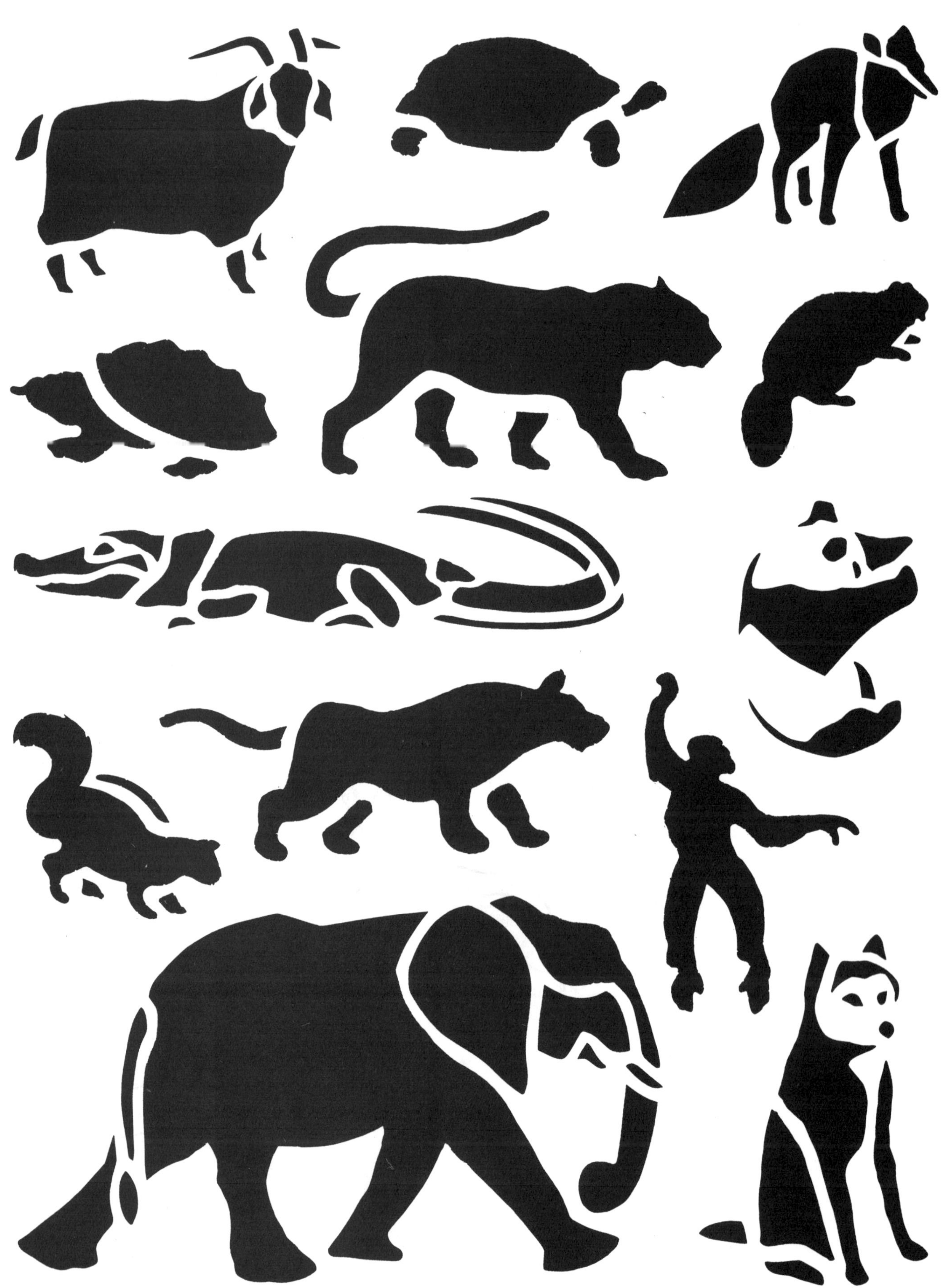

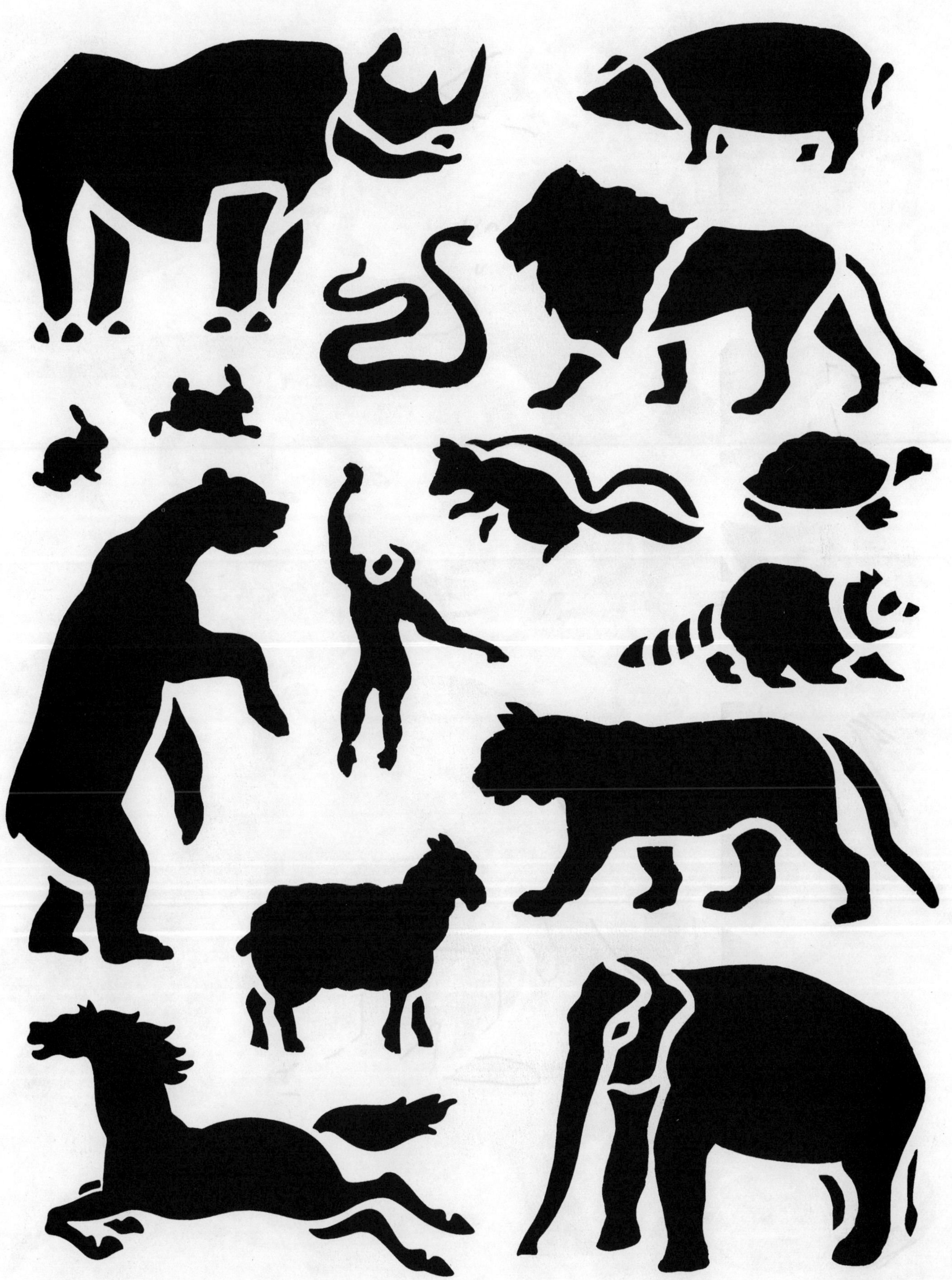

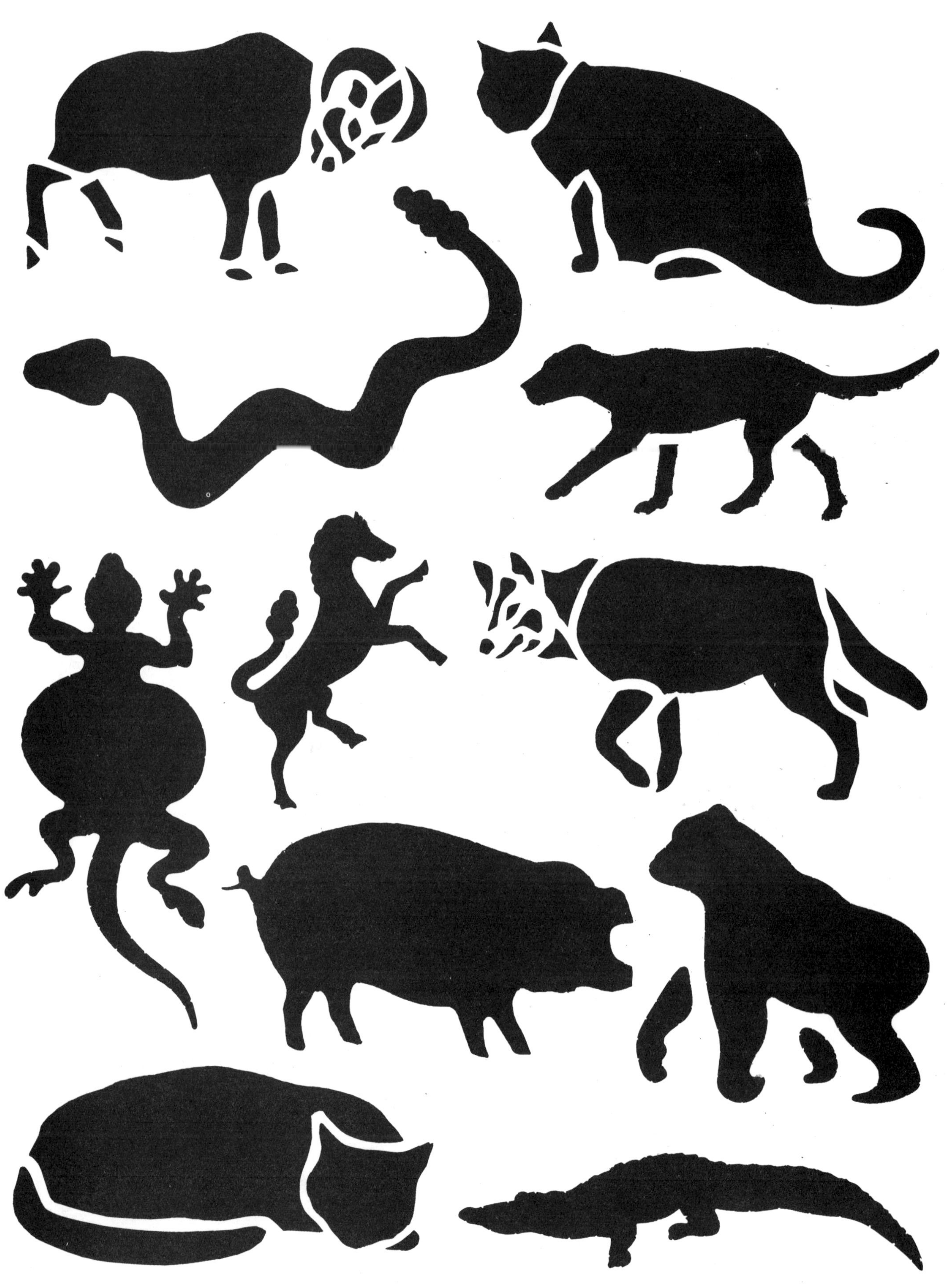

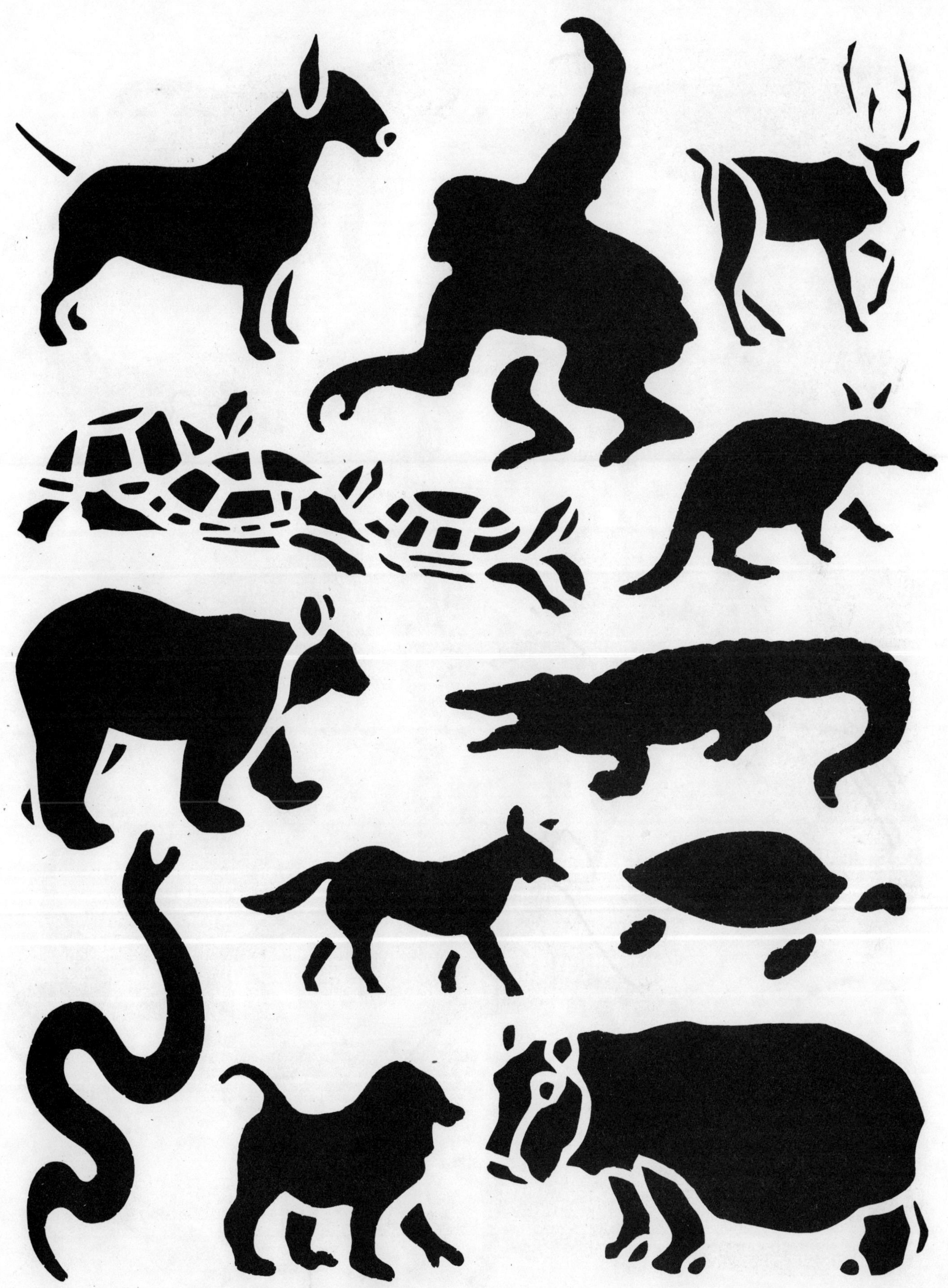

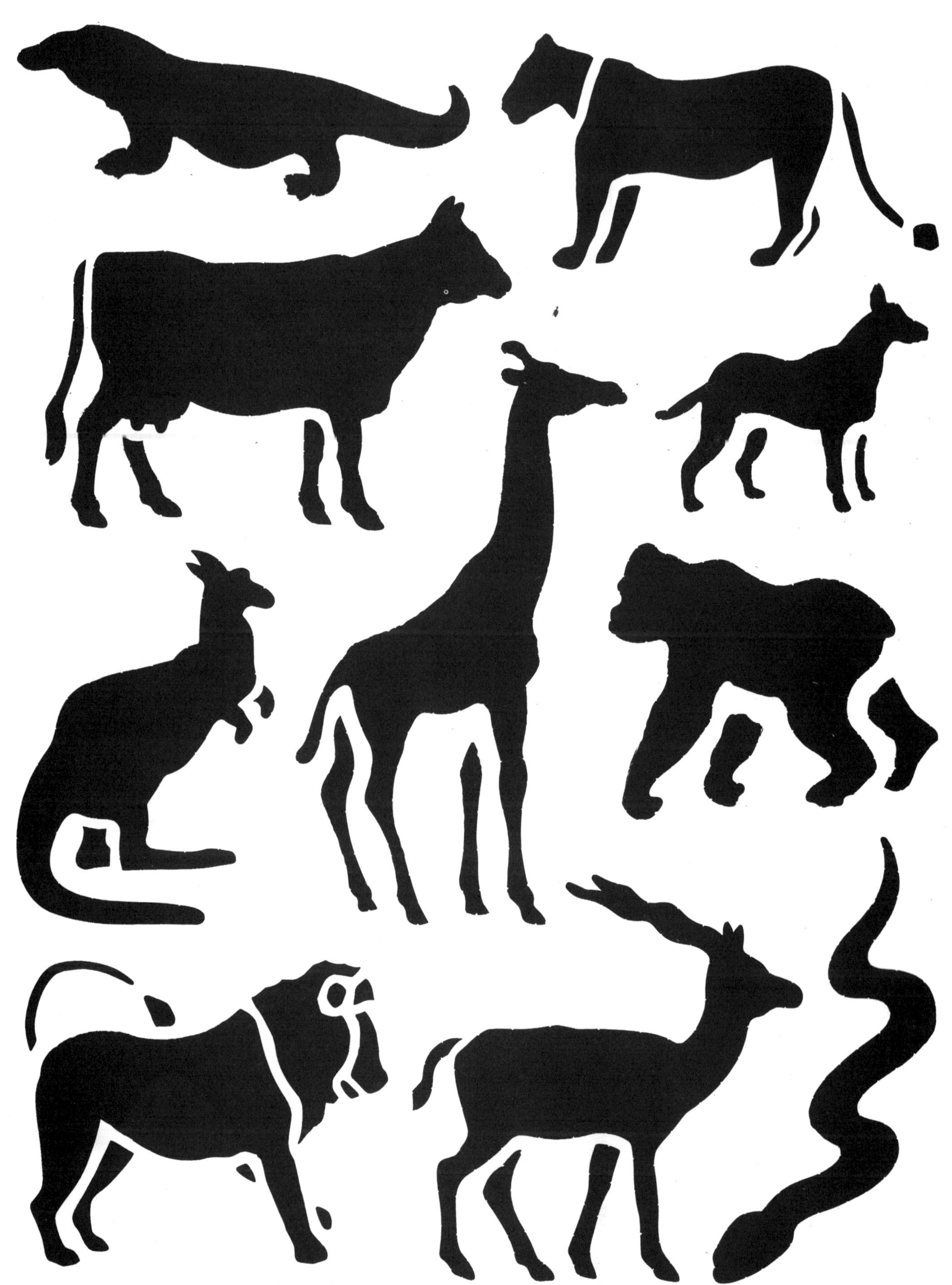

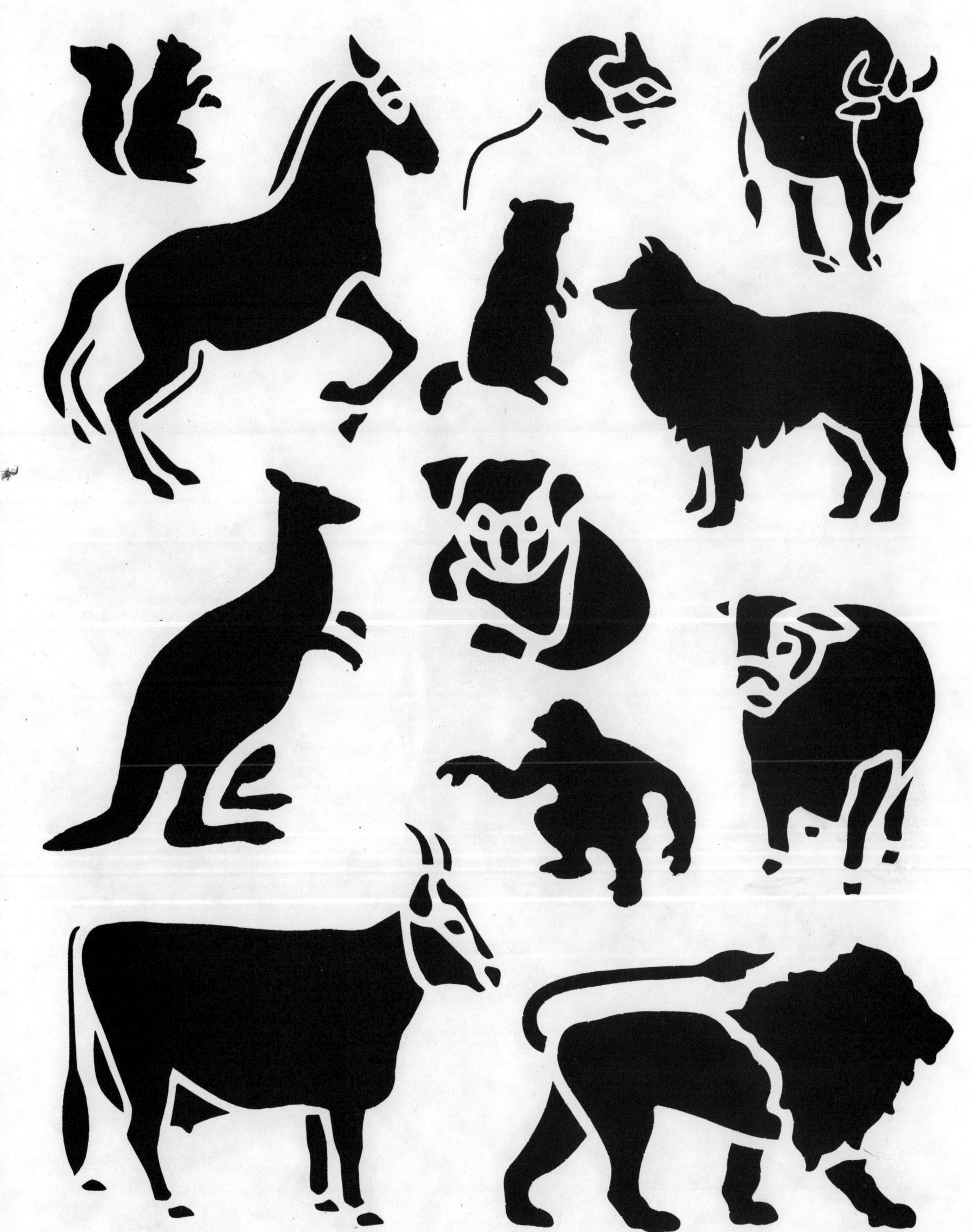

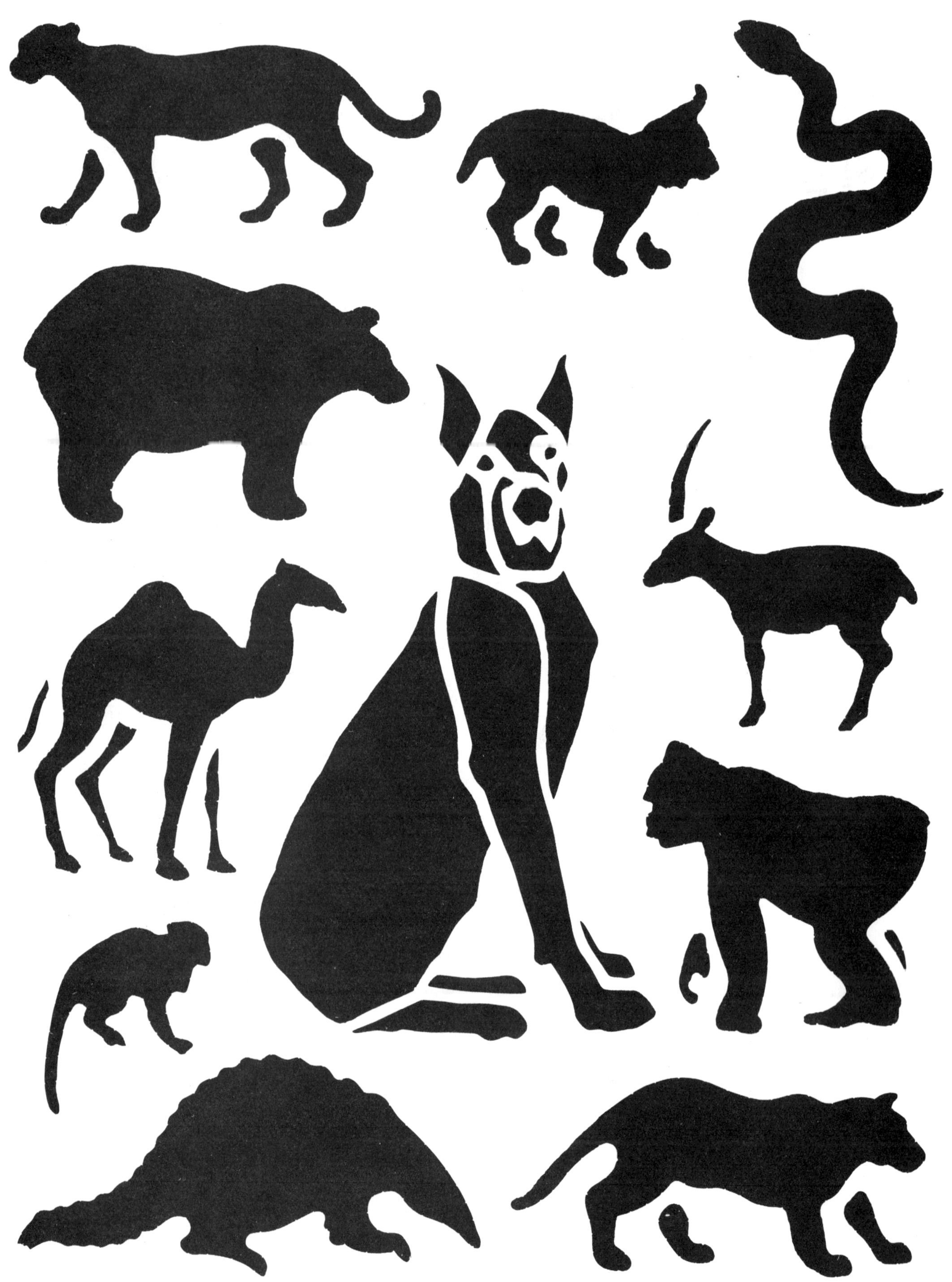

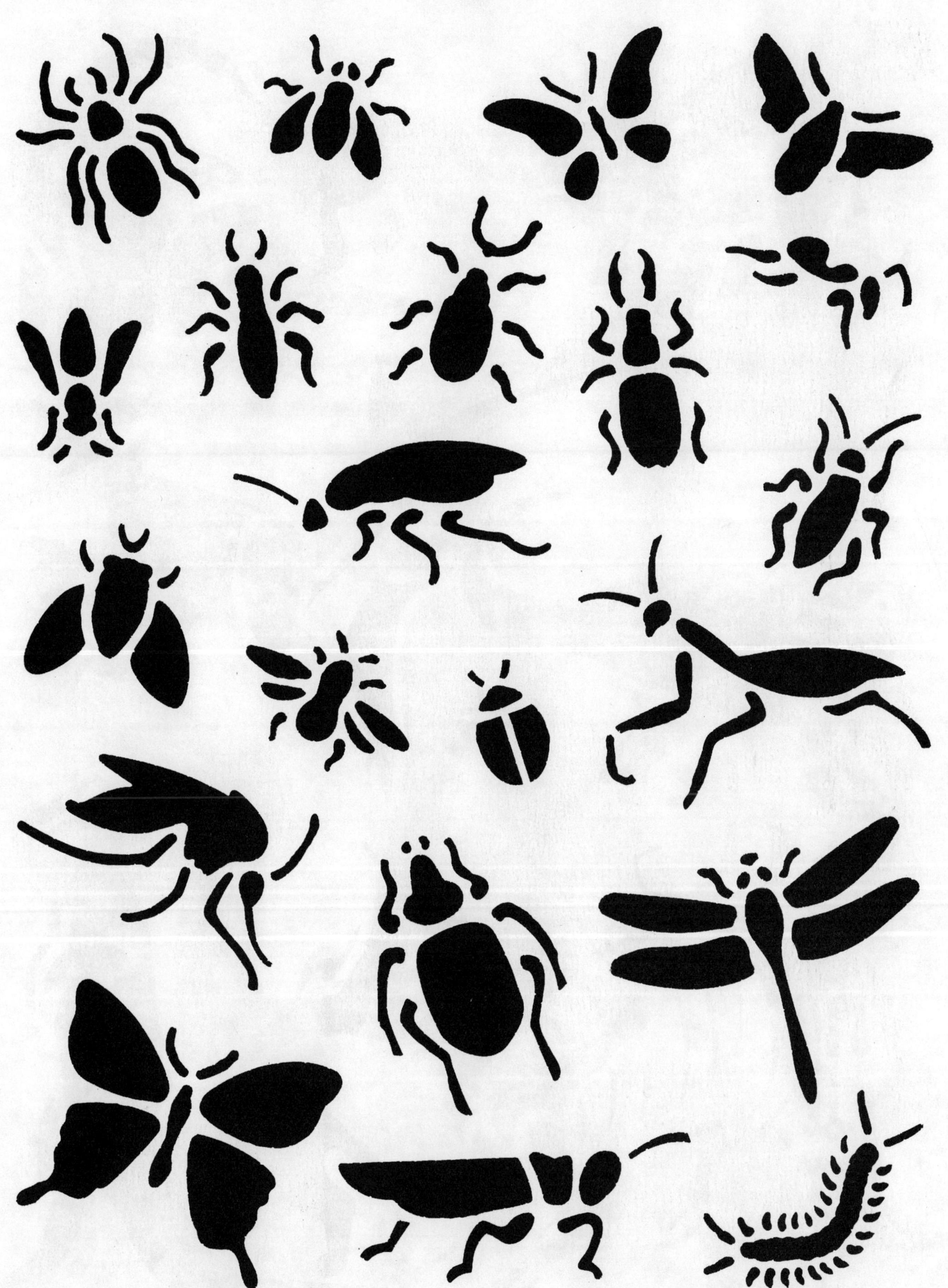

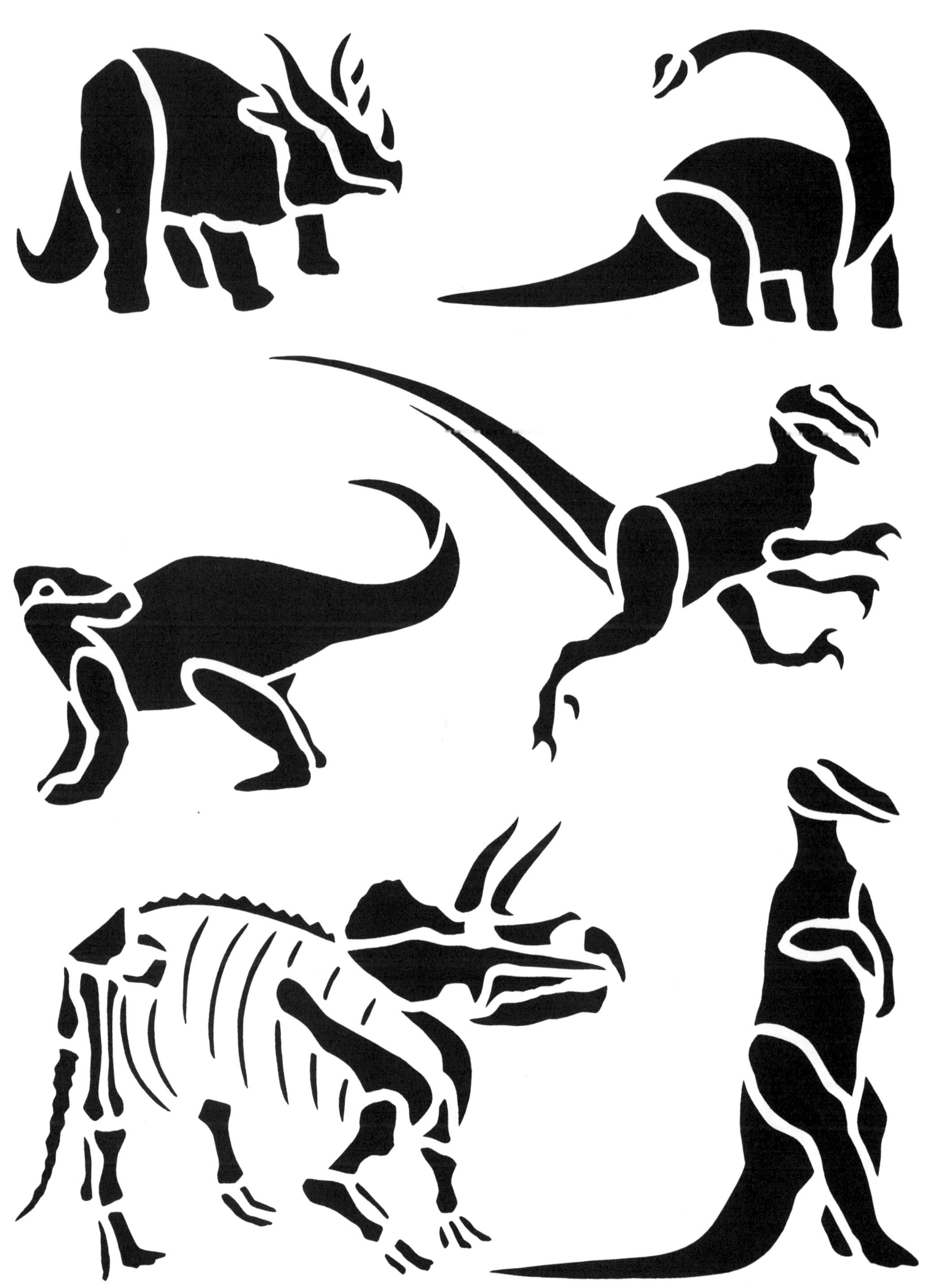

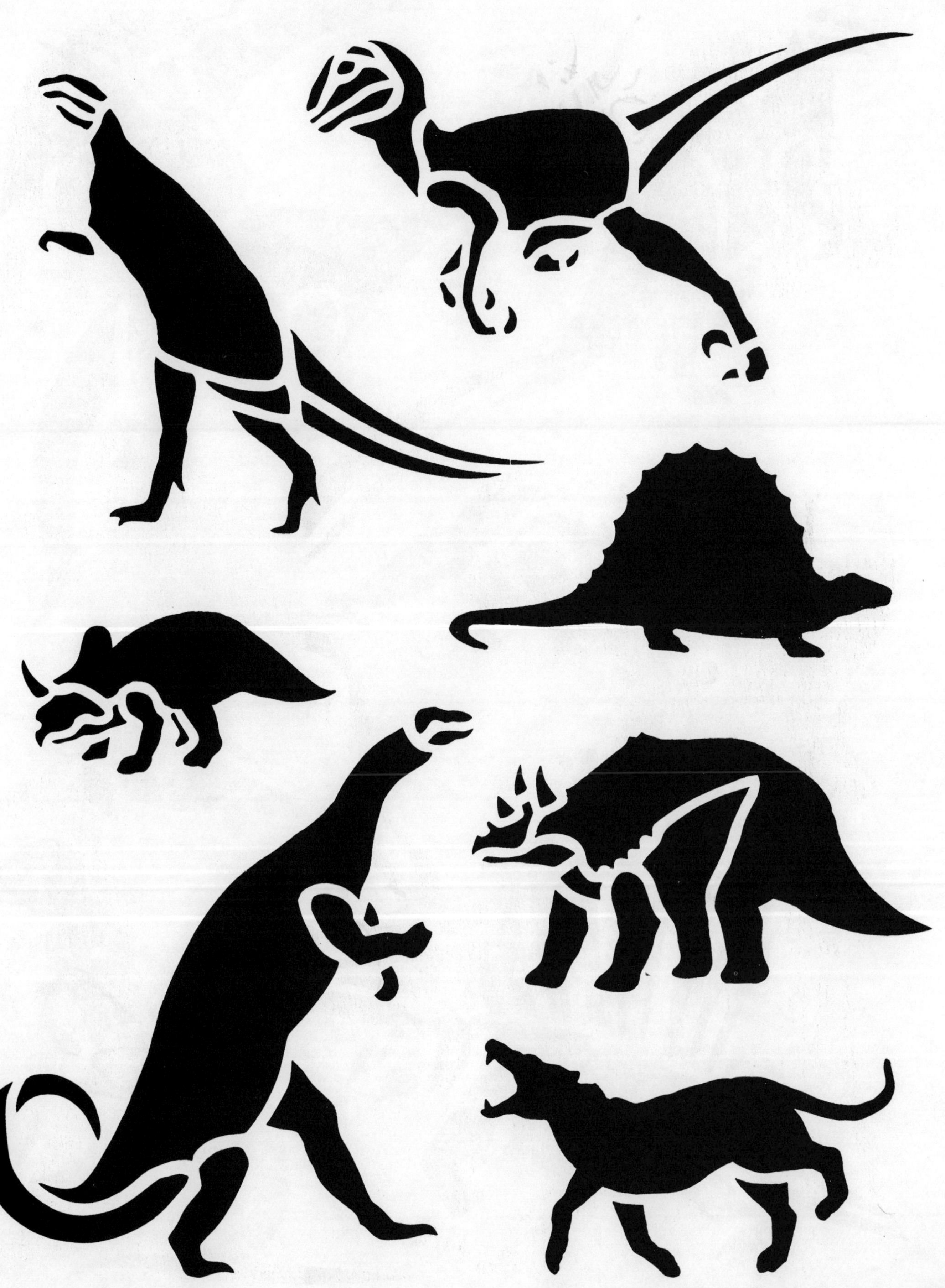

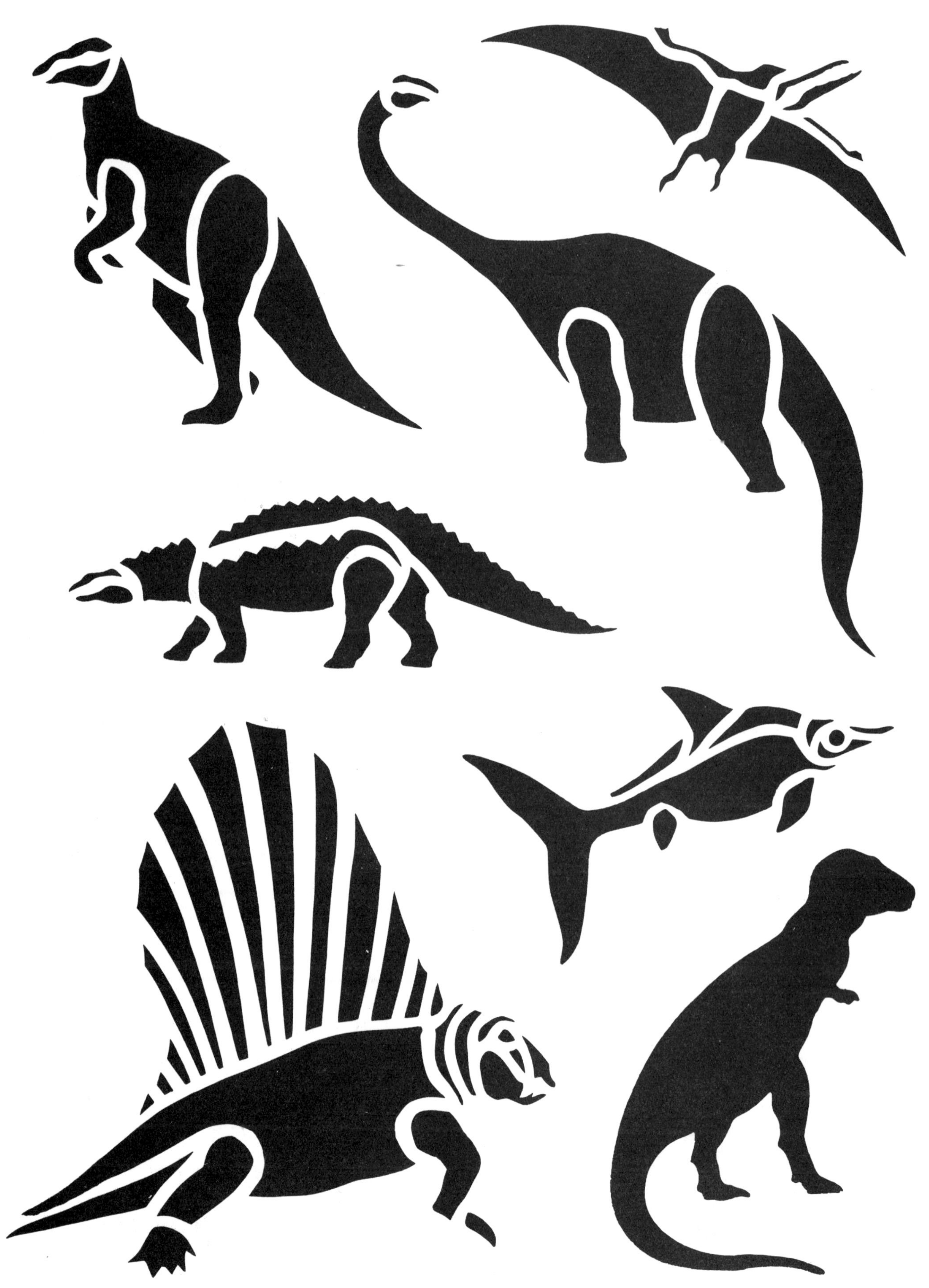

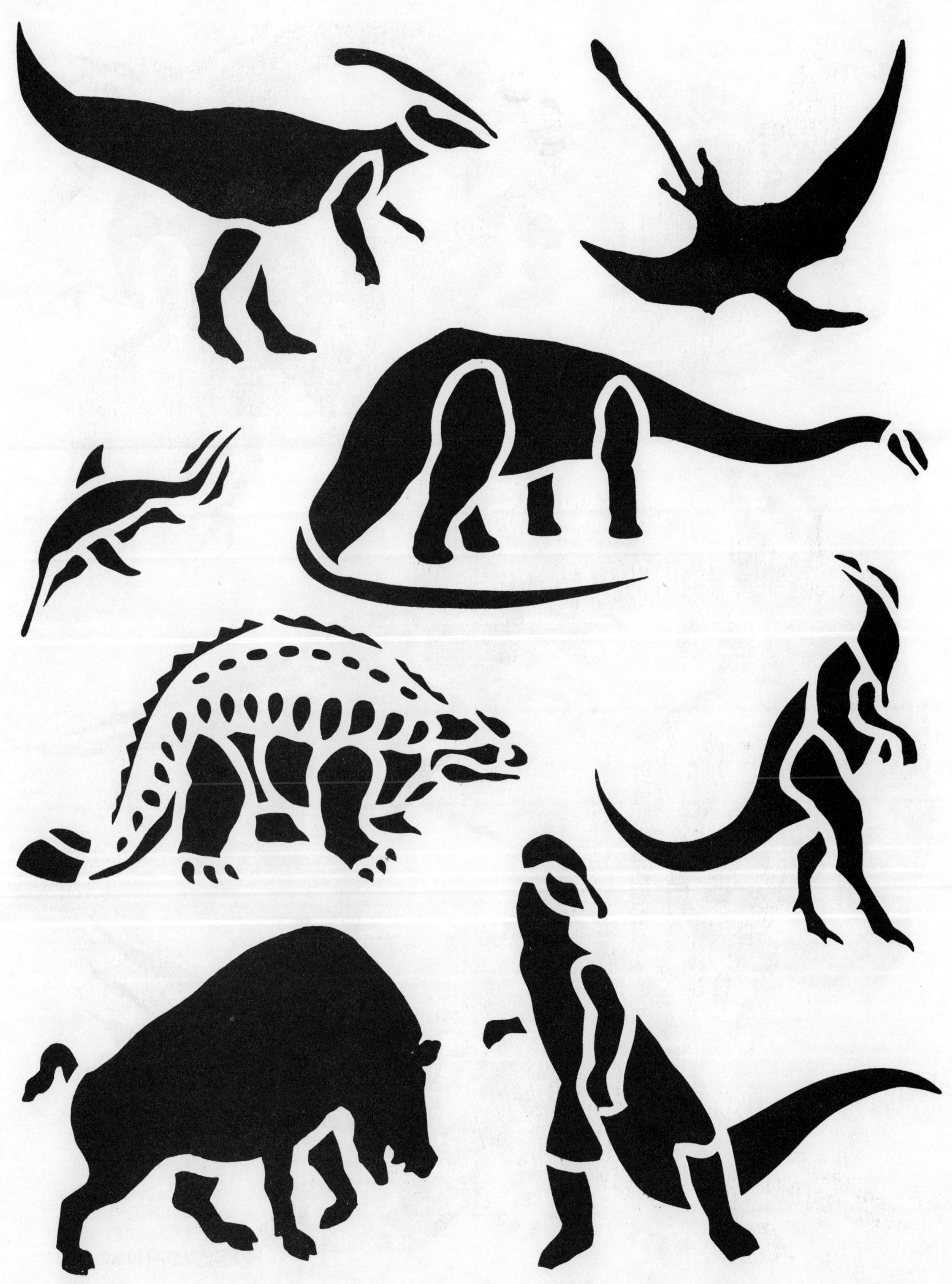

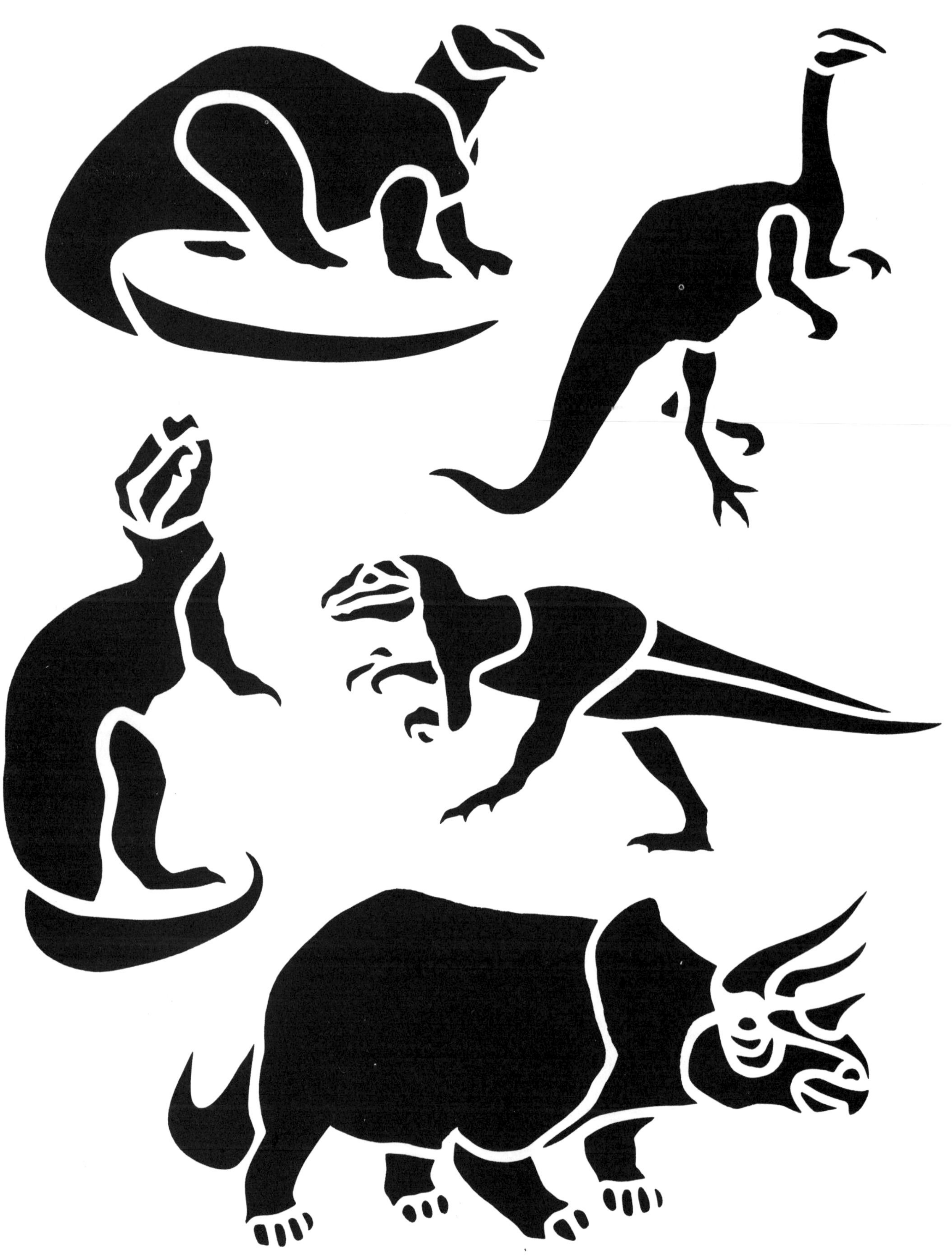

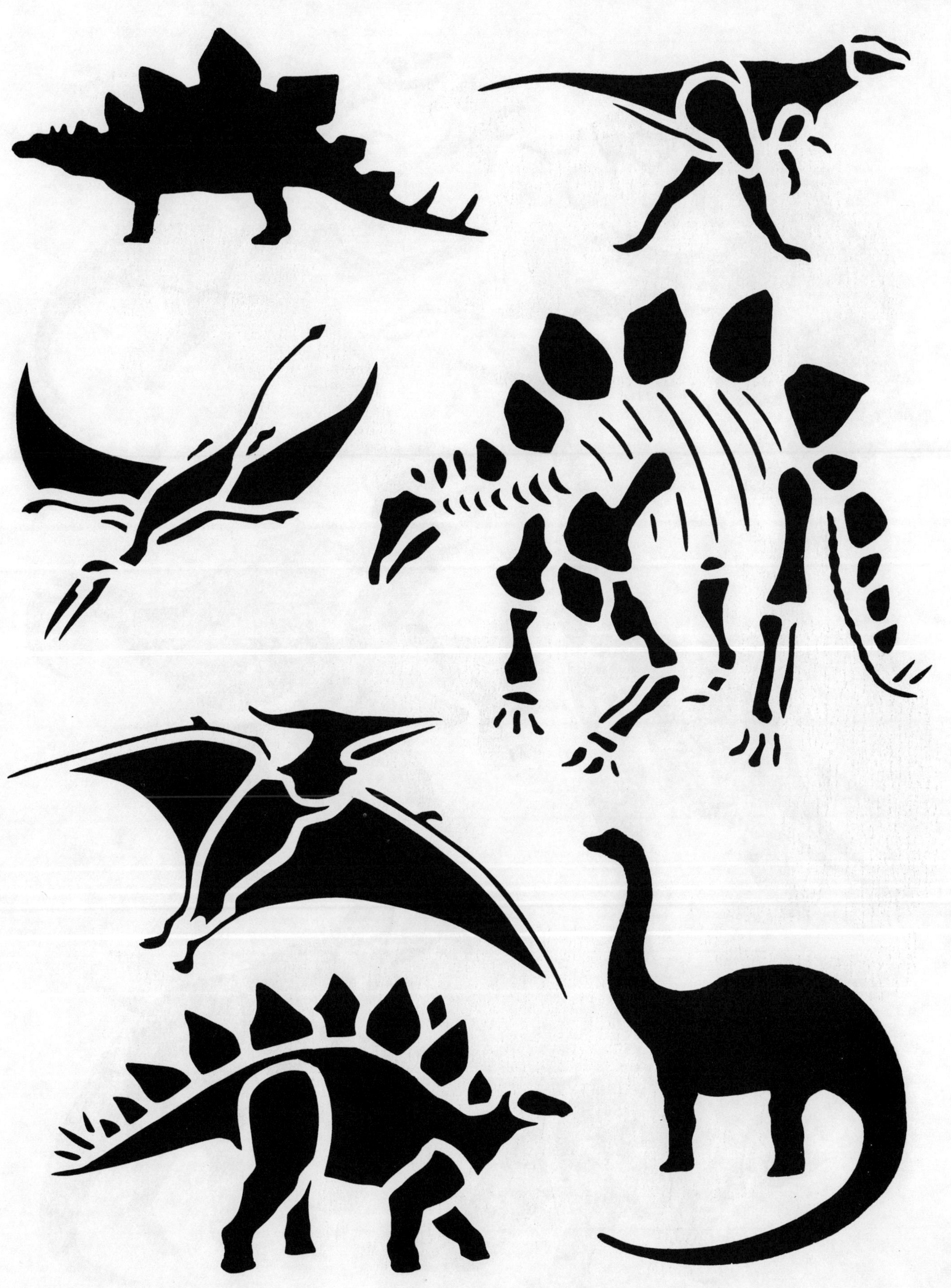

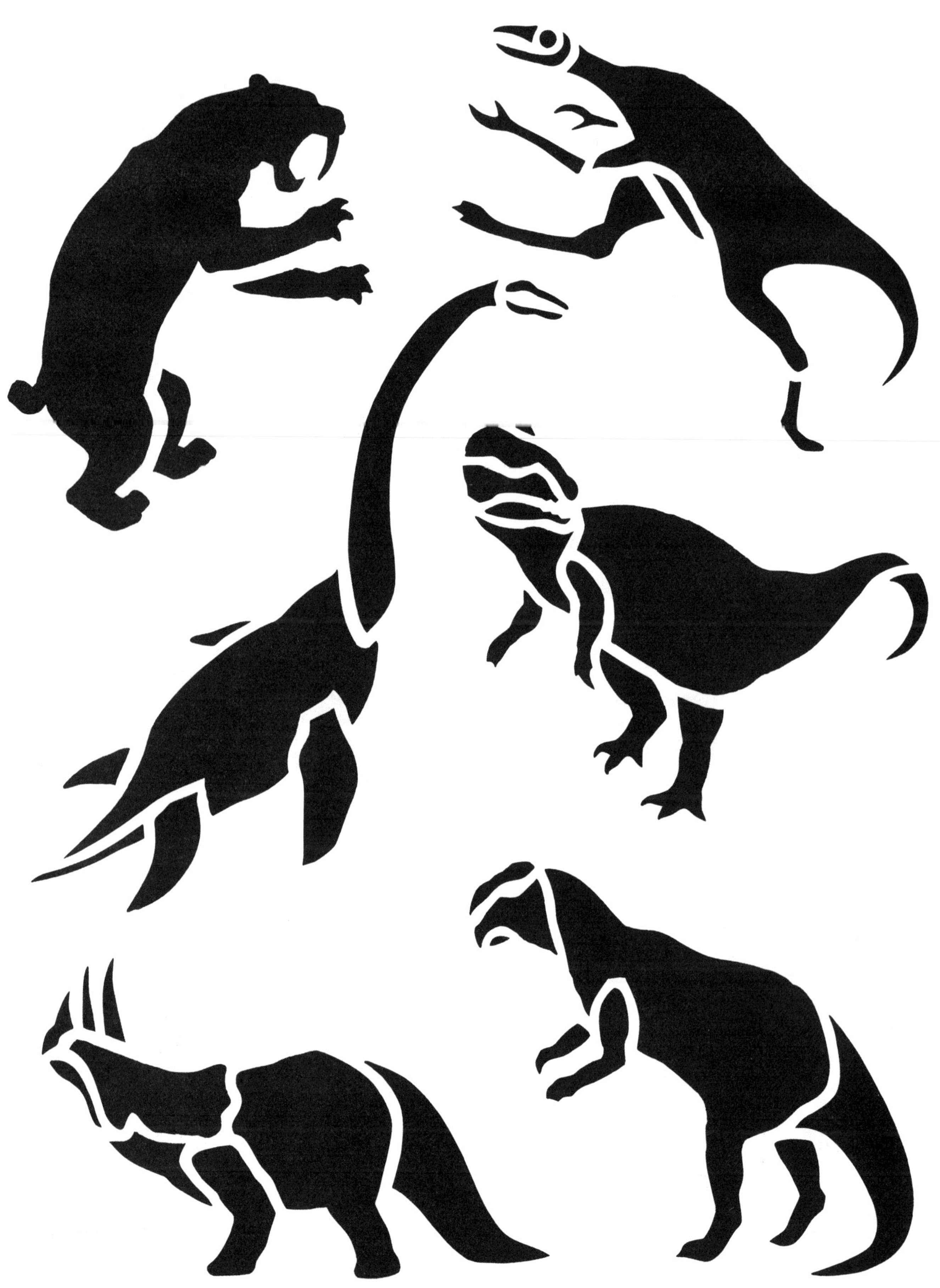

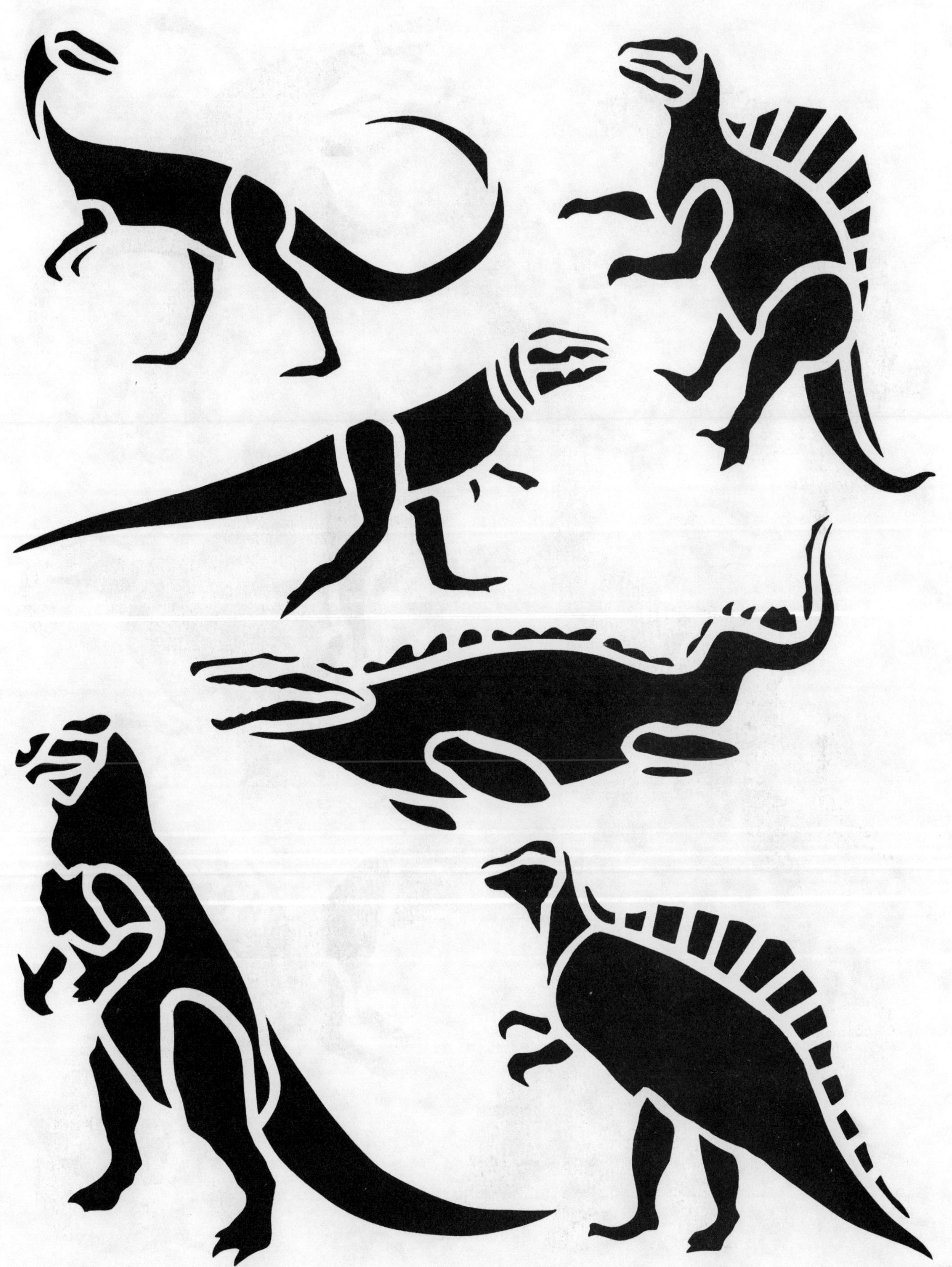

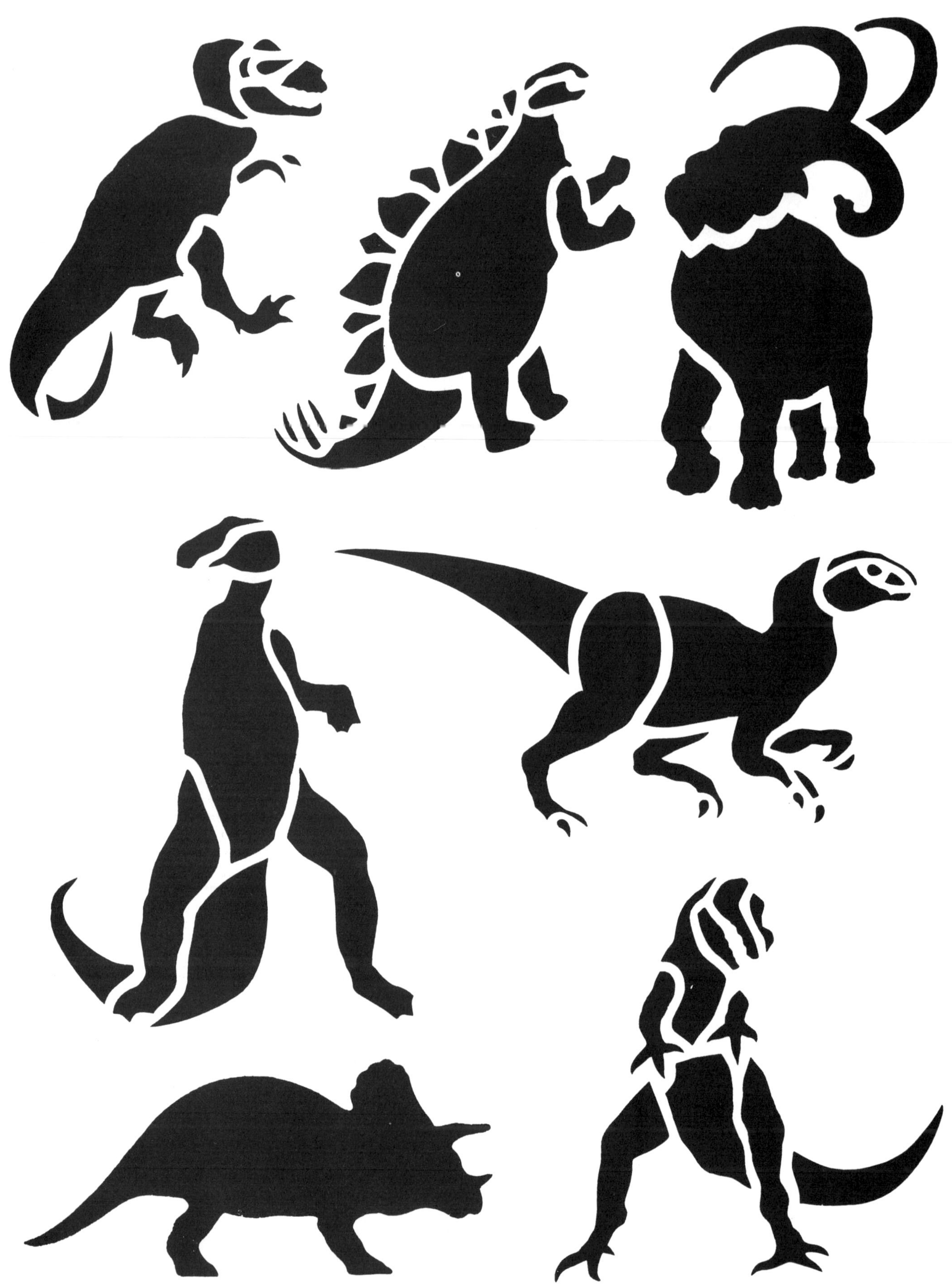

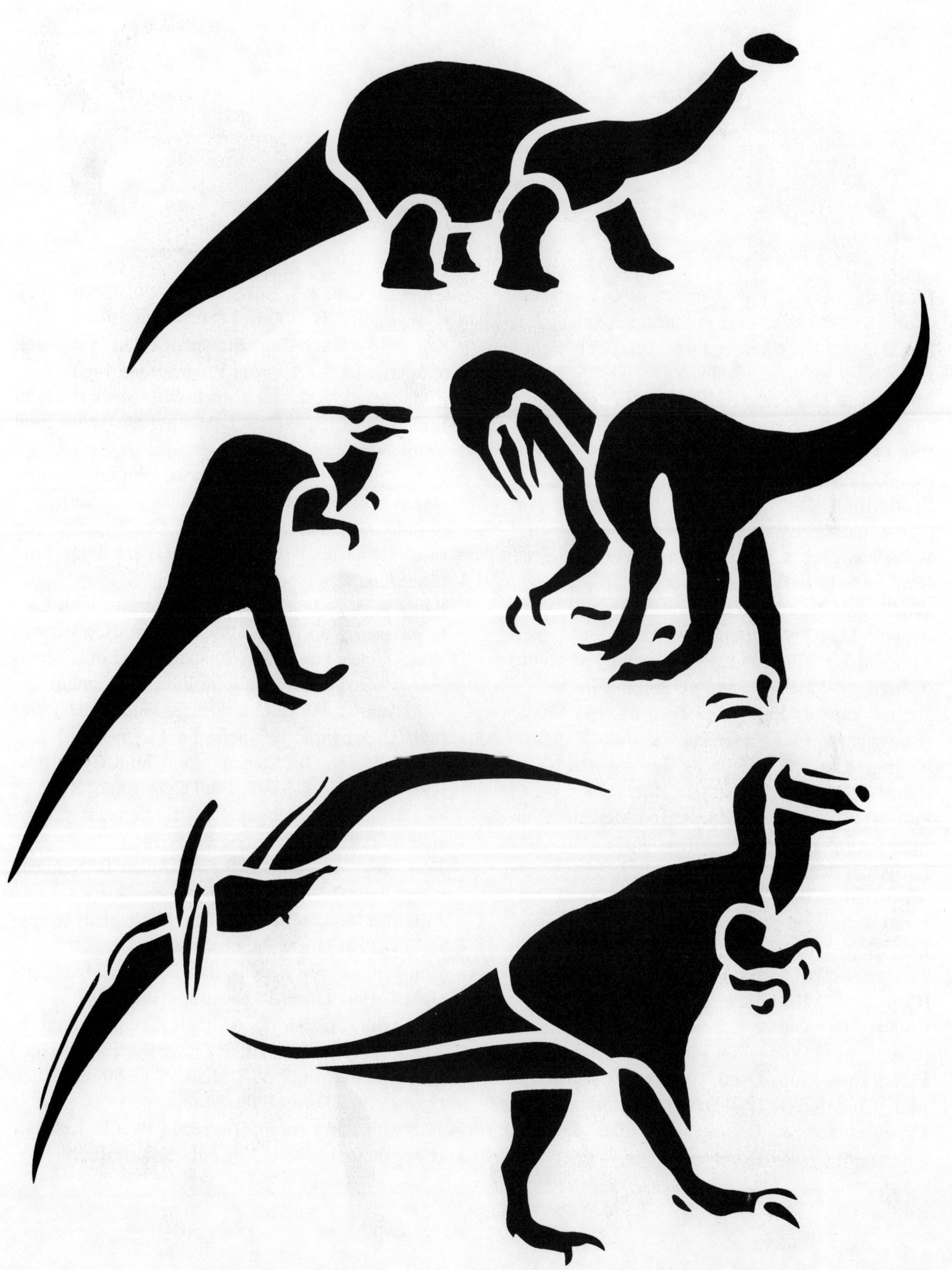

Sources of the Designs

Floral Borders Cut & Use Stencils, Ed Sibbett (Copyright © 1986 Dover Publications, Inc.)
Floral Cut & Use Stencils, Ed Sibbett (Copyright © 1979 Dover Publications, Inc.)
Bird Cut & Use Stencils, Ed Sibbett (Copyright © 1981 Dover Publications, Inc.)
Roses Cut & Use Stencils, Celeste Plowden (Copyright © 1994 Celeste Plowden)
Exotic Birds Cut & Use Stencils, Celeste Plowden (Copyright © 1993 Celeste Plowden)
Waterfowl Cut & Use Stencils, Celeste Plowden (Copyright © 1993 Celeste Plowden)
Wildflowers Cut & Use Stencils, Celeste Plowden (Copyright © 1992 Celeste Plowden)
Fish and Sea Life Cut & Use Stencils, Ted Menten (Copyright © 1983 Dover Publications, Inc.)
Animal Friends Punch-Out Stencils, Ted Menten (Copyright © 1985 Dover Publications, Inc.)
Nautical Cut & Use Stencils, Ted Menten (Copyright © 1986 Dover Publications, Inc.)
Folk Art Cut & Use Stencils, Ted Menten (Copyright © 1985 Dover Publications, Inc.)
Early American Cut & Use Stencils, JoAnne C. Day (Copyright © 1975 Dover Publications, Inc.)
Pennsylvania Dutch Cut & Use Stencils, JoAnne C. Day (Copyright © 1975 Dover Publications, Inc.)
Country Design Cut & Use Stencils, M. Jane Baker (Copyright © 1984 M. Jane Baker)
Country Life Cut & Use Stencils, Ellen Sandbeck (Copyright © 1990 Dover Publications, Inc.)
Flowers and Fruits Cut & Use Stencils, Ellen Sandbeck (Copyright © 1990 Dover Publications, Inc.)
Dinosaur Cut & Use Stencils, Ellen Sandbeck (Copyright © 1989 Dover Publications, Inc.)
Animals Cut & Use Stencils, Ellen Sandbeck (Copyright © 1988 Dover Publications, Inc.)
Sea Life Punch-Out Stencils, Ellen Sandbeck (Copyright © 1991 Dover Publications, Inc.)
Endangered Animals Punch-Out Stencils, John Emil Cymerman (Copyright © 1996 John Emil Cymerman)
Farm Animals Punch-Out Stencils, John Emil Cymerman (Copyright © 1993 John Emil Cymerman)
Reptiles and Amphibians Punch-Out Stencils, John Emil Cymerman (Copyright © 1993 John Emil Cymerman)
Rain Forest Animals Punch-Out Stencils, John Emil Cymerman (Copyright © 1995 John Emil Cymerman)
Zoo Animals Punch-Out Stencils, John Emil Cymerman (Copyright © 1992 John Emil Cymerman)
Wild Animals Punch-Out Stencils, John Emil Cymerman (Copyright © 1994 John Emil Cymerman)
Insects Punch-Out Stencils, John Emil Cymerman (Copyright © 1994 John Emil Cymerman)
Fun with Trees Stencils, Paul E. Kennedy (Copyright © 1992 Dover Publications, Inc.)
Fun with Zoo Animals Stencils, Paul E. Kennedy (Copyright © 1989 Dover Publications, Inc.)
Fun with Reptiles Stencils, Paul E. Kennedy (Copyright © 1994 Dover Publications, Inc.)
Fun with Leaves Stencils, Paul E. Kennedy (Copyright © 1991 Dover Publications, Inc.)
Fun with Prehistoric Animals Stencils, Paul E. Kennedy (Copyright © 1996 Dover Publications, Inc.)
Fun with Favorite Pets Stencils, A. G. Smith (Copyright © 1987 Dover Publications, Inc.)
Fun with Farm Animals Stencils, Paul E. Kennedy (Copyright © 1988 Dover Publications, Inc.)